Danse Macabre

Danse Macabre

*Thoughts on Death and Memento Mori
from a Hospice Chaplain*

N. THOMAS JOHNSON-MEDLAND

RESOURCE *Publications* • Eugene, Oregon

DANSE MACABRE
Thoughts on Death and Memento Mori from a Hospice Chaplain

Copyright © 2011 N. Thomas Johnson-Medland. All rights reserved. Except for brief quotations in critical publications or reviews, no part of this book may be reproduced in any manner without prior written permission from the publisher. Write: Permissions, Wipf and Stock Publishers, 199 W. 8th Ave., Suite 3, Eugene, OR 97401.

Resource Publications
An Imprint of Wipf and Stock Publishers
199 W. 8th Ave., Suite 3
Eugene, OR 97401
www.wipfandstock.com

ISBN 13: 978-1-61097-577-3
Manufactured in the U.S.A.

All scripture quotations, unless otherwise indicated, are taken from the Holy Bible, New International Version®, NIV®. Copyright ©1973, 1978, 1984 by Biblica, Inc.™ Used by permission of Zondervan. All rights reserved worldwide.

This book is dedicated to Mom-Mom who used to tease the daylights out of me with her wonderful sense of humor, to Pop-Pop whose depth of character is embedded in my soul; and, to my paternal grandparents whom I never knew. I still reach out to all of you in my living. You are a part of this in a very real way.

"Remember the day of your death. See what the death of your body will be like. Let your spirit be heavy, take pains, condemn the vanity of the world, so as to be able to live always in the peace you have in view without weakening."

—Abba Evagrios, "The Apophthegmata Patrum"

"God changes his appearance every second. Blessed is the man who can recognize him in all his disguises."

—Nikos Kazantzakis, "Zorba the Greek"

"A person needs a little madness, or else they never dare cut the rope and be free."

—Nikos Kazantzakis, "Zorba the Greek"

"Depend upon it, sir, when a man knows he is to be hanged in a fortnight, it concentrates his mind wonderfully."
—Samuel Johnson, "Boswell: Life"

"That we must all die, we always knew; I wish I had remembered it sooner."

—Samuel Johnson, "Letter to Sir Joshua Reynolds"

Contents

Acknowledgments ix
Preface xi
Introduction xiii

Chapter One / 1

Chapter Two / 14

Chapter Three / 23

Chapter Four / 27

Chapter Five / 32

Chapter Six / 41

Chapter Seven / 51

Chapter Eight / 61

Chapter Nine / 67

Chapter Ten / 71

Chapter Eleven / 78

Chapter Twelve / 86

Chapter Thirteen / 91

Chapter Fourteen / 94

Chapter Fifteen / 163

Acknowledgments

THANK YOU to all of the hospice patients and their families I have had the good pleasure to serve. Your open integrity as individuals helped reveal the common nature to all of our suffering: we are all in need of love. Sometimes I cannot believe the things that you revealed to me about the wonder and awe that lie under every stone and every piece of dust in this life. Life is itself amazing; death seems to be a continuation of that same amazement. I have felt you all in my life at one time or another.

Thank you Elisabeth for always causing me to think. There is always one more perspective and one more vantage point from which to view things from. You helped me to discover these by teaching me to listen and to hear; to look and to see.

And, thank you to the Centennial School District in Bucks County, PA for showing us the filmstrip "Danse Macabre" every year at Halloween. Apparently, it changed my life. View the filmstrip at: http://www.youtube.com/watch?v=Vd0w4L5i828

Preface

DANSE MACABRE is a manuscript I have been writing—off and on—over the years in my work with the dying. I began to realize that modern man is hidden behind a series of fears when it comes to death. Part of this comes from lack of knowledge, part from failure to discuss death.

In the advent of the splintering of religion and faith (into denominations and sects) there is no one solid or consistent dogmatic approach that is held or taught across the whole of a religious or faith-based society. The great Catholic, Byzantine and Ottoman Empires (to name a few) had massive structural programs of belief and practice that unified them over space and time. Most often they used laws to maintain an epic and whole system.

This splintering has occurred in all faiths; in all religions, and in all cultures. This is true with every major religion and sect in America, as well as around the globe. It is also true with every culture, ethnicity, and gathering of people. The splintering of faiths, cultures, ethnicities, and gatherings into factions allows for an immensely divergent stream of thought and belief to emerge from the new diversity. It also poses conflict. This is true surrounding the stories we tell about death—our beliefs.

The experiment of the American melting-pot of cultures (faiths, ethnicities, and gatherings, too) has also added a more diverse population to the social/cultural mix and discussion of "death and dying in America". We live and thrive with people of many faiths and many factions within those faiths; with many cultures and many sub-cultures within those cultures. This immense and rich milieu of religion and culture adds layers of complexity to some of the silence surrounding death, as we fear intruding or

Preface

causing arguments. Add to that the sudden onslaught of information from every known corner of the globe as a result of our invasive and all pervading technologies in the digital age. We can know anything and be anywhere all of the time.

How are we to live in a multi-cultured society with layer upon layer of divergent belief surrounding us at every turn? How are we to share a common life in such close proximity with immense disparities—immense disparities that are worldwide and all inclusive. We are continually barraged with news from the entire hamlet or village, but that hamlet has become the universe, that village the cosmos. That is huge.

The work I have compiled is my own rendering of my days while taking care of dying people. I was involved in the spiritual care of dying patients and their families for almost twelve years. These words and these stories come from the work I did in and among them. I have added my own personal forays into dealing with personal deaths in my own life. I have also added my own thoughts around my own dying. I have carried, what I can, into the discussion that comes from the panoply of cultures I entered into in the care of the dying.

My hope is that these candid and simple stories about death will enable individuals and communities (families and faiths, and people with no faith) to begin to talk about the mythologies they share about death. It is also my hope that it will open communities to sensing where the need for healing exists in our lives with death. Surely, we are dancing with death throughout the whole of our lives.

Introduction

I WONDER why when every single human being on the planet—and every other living thing as well—is moving closer and closer to death, we do not talk about death more often. I also wonder why we do not spend more time trying to make our deaths more meaningful.

For the most part, we spend our time avoiding death at all costs, and avoiding any mention of or thought about its reality. But you know it has got to be impacting everything we do or think. Just because we do not mention something or process that thing verbally does not mean that that thing will not drive and inform everything we do. All it means is that it will drive it and inform it from the subconscious world. From that place, we are less likely to gain power over our fears. From that place—the subconscious—we are more likely to be eaten alive by the dragons we have repressed.

∼ ∼ ∼

The idea of death stalks us at every turn.

∼ ∼ ∼

It may actually be Death Himself that stalks us at every turn.

∼ ∼ ∼

Whether it is the idea of death or Death Himself, it does not matter. We are stalked throughout our whole lives by the notion, the idea, the feeling, the reality and the imminent haunting dream that we are going to "not be alive" someday. Someday, what we are now will either not be at all or will somehow be different—very different. Someday we will die.

Introduction

We are stalked by this at every turn. We are all stalked by this and yet we fail to talk about being stalked. We live in a silent fear and collusion when it comes to death: "I won't talk about it if you don't."

It is time that we talk about death and the fact that we will all die.

I have been swimming through words my whole life. They have been under me, over me, and even within me. Everything—even until now—has been a ripple on the surface of their water; a disturbance in their force; a means of waking me up. Everything has led up to this "now". All of the words, emotions, experiences, and processes that I have seen and handled and lived among coalesce to make me who I am. All that stuff is still in me. Some of those words are about death.

I believe words are a gift for us to use to add meaning to the things we have experienced. Words are a gift to help us unite with other people; unite behind words that can reveal that we are very much the same with some slight variations that make us different. Words are bridges to the separateness among us that makes us one.

A new universe explodes into consciousness every moment in cosmic time. Pieces of God wake up to remembrance, every time an eye opens to the morning. The whole of creation swims in words and is awakened to itself with every fluttering breath. Each time someone is aware, God has a breath.

In this scenario death is but the closing of an eye. Life is but the opening of consciousness to what it means to be awake—awake and with words. "Now" is life and being awake. This moment has death just beside it, just next to it. But, this moment is itself life.

Introduction

Words can help us paint simple and exotic images about the encounters we have and the meaning of these encounters. Words can help us encounter death and uncover the meaning it has in life. We would need to sound those words, first. Then, we would need to share them. This would require we lay down the silent fear and collusion we have surrounding words about death.

Being with over 1500 hospice patients and their families during the approach of death, I have seen again and again how bringing words up and out of the darkness of our interior lives and into the light of day, helps to make us whole and integrated. We are healthier when we are able to allow these things to come up and out of us, and not repress them inside forever.

Somehow we have lost our words about dying. We have stopped having meaningful discussion and elaborate myths about what goes on and how things unwind. Death has become the great silence. It is a place and a journey we refuse to utter.

I started out wanting to just tell you stories about death from hospice patients and their families. Then I realized that death was tied to every assumption and hope that we have as human beings and that we would end up having to discuss the dozens of layers of meaning in our lives because death was attached to all of them— death is attached to everything. Death and the idea of death drives everything we do or think or say or that we fail to do or think or say. I guess that may be why we go mute about the subject.

Death is attached to everything.

Bear with me, the conversation will become muddled. We not only want to avoid the topic, but when we do talk about it, the air gets thick with confusion.

Introduction

Perhaps it is because death uncovers the great fear in all of us. Perhaps it is because we are unprepared for how death will approach us. Perhaps it is because we are not sure if our stories of death are right or wrong; or if their stories about death are more right or more wrong. Whatever the reason, we do not talk about death much—if at all. And yet, death is a way we must all go.

Our neighbors may not hold the same set of words about what death means. We believe our death is a bursting into resurrection. They believe our death is a becoming of dirt. The other ones—over there—believe that our death is just another way to get back in line to come back to life as something else. Rather than just allowing multiple stories about how things may go; it is just better not to talk about it. Or so we believe.

We have gotten silent about a lot of things because of this diversity. Who wants to discuss their looming fears with people who have such divergent beliefs? Why risk? But we are going to encounter the rich diversity of belief and story more frequently these days as our technology has made us one village, one people almost overnight. We have had no time to figure out how to live in this new reality.

If we get silent in the face of this great fear, we pass nothing on to our progeny or our surviving race about what it is we are feeling. We deny them the ability to know what is normal in human experience. This kind of silence robs mankind of depth. It is not the silence of contemplation and love. It is the silence of fear. Speaking into the fear is often enough to lift the heaviness of its pall. Not just for us, but for all who come after.

The fear is not simply about feeling unprepared to die, or sharing divergent beliefs about death. The fear is also about feeling unprepared to talk about, contemplate, feel anything about death itself; unprepared because we have not allowed ourselves to playfully and routinely regard death (let alone the mystery of living). In light of this global village of information that we have been thrust

Introduction

into overnight, what could I possibly add to the discussion around death—or anything for that matter?

This uncovers another fear, the fear that talking about death will cause death to happen. Just listen to how people soften their voice to a whisper when they say the words: "cancer", "death", "terminal". The very sound of the words makes us shutter. We impose magic on the words. Magic that does not bear out in principle. Magic that is tied to fear.

The only sure thing that will come to pass in the life of anything born is that it will die. Living things die. That death hides behind the silence of a myriad of fears.

Swimming along side and just to the rear of these fears is the fear that hides behind them—pushing them out into plain view. It is the fear of living; the fear of truly being alive. The fear of living hides behind the fear of contemplating or communicating death and the fear of hastening death. It will not let us live because it fears making too much noise in the presence of death. As if it would become a target of death itself. Having a "Zorba-like ethos" or "joy of living mentality" somehow taunts death and all of the other dark, negative forces and attributes of life. If you enjoy life too much, it will surely be taken from you.

Without a regard for death, without bringing it up, without truly living we will never be able to be awaken and live in the now. Our fears of death keep us already dead. Numbed, we sit behind a curtain, viewing death and calling it life. How have we become so mixed up? Why do we choose to live with unresolved fears?

It is time to carve out some words about death. It is time to uncover some of our fears and look at this thing that will affect all of us.

Introduction

I will place some words I have found and some words I have formed into a space with enough room around them so we can look at them and see them clearly. Perhaps gain visual access to some notions we had never seen before; maybe hear something old in a new way. Maybe be able to dispel a thing or two that does not fit.

We have become a global village very quickly. We can know way too much, way too quickly. With the onslaught of constant information we have lost our ability to process and lost the time we need to be able to process all of the things we now are able to know in an instant. We need to sit back and craft some words and tell some tales about the things we now are able to know. We need to process the immense world we have at our fingertips twenty four hours every day.

We have not always made the best choices in how to deal with this much omniscience in this short amount of time. It would be good to take this seriously. Maybe we can do some of that here.

∽ ∽ ∽

We need to make some words about death and our fears of death; and, we need to share them.

∽ ∽ ∽

It may be their first showing for some of us. The words about death and the fear of death, that is. Others will simply be seeing them again—yet anew. Whether we are able to remove those fears we have uttered above will be up to our tenacity—the tenacity of an engaged and steadily paced reader. My job will be to be faithful to giving up new and used words about death; words with ample space for the viewing and feeling. Words that will call you out into the open—for just a bit—to be exposed to potentially new and awkward ways of putting words together; and, along with that, new and awkward ways to put ideas and beliefs together as well.

If our words can help us to remove some of our fears, we will have climbed to the top of the mountain of what it means to be human. We will have summated a critical obstacle.

Introduction

Many people will take shots at what I say. My aim is to lure you into the conversation; so I am ready for the dialogue that comes with that.

"Memento mori" is Latin for remembering our death. Remembering that we will someday die—perhaps even today—can build will and passion into our lives. Remembering that we will die can cause us to live by reminding us that we will not always have the opportunity to live.

The desert ascetics were often quoted as saying "Remember your Death." It became watchwords of the mystical desert experience. Do everything as if you were going to die today. Keep that reality before you as a guide for helping you to make choices. Be prepared to enter the final act, give a good performance. This was a way of talking about death.

When I first heard this aphorism—"remember your death"—I thought it was the tragic mantra of under-sexed monks. I figured that their life without physical intimacy had caused them to go mad and that they moved ahead in life on the wings of their own fears, repressions, and bitterness. Physical abstinence had caused these folks a morbid depression—sort of sounding pious. I have come to know that that was not the case. Remembering our death is a valuable way to live.

Death is nothing but a transformation of the seed into the plant and the plant back into the seed. It is the leaf becoming the dirt and the dirt becoming leaf. It is the heart becoming spirit and the spirit becoming heart. It is man becoming anew in every possible way that he can.

We would do well to remember that this sort of change is coming for all of us. This change is coming; and, what it is that lies on the other side of this change is not something that we know about with exactitude or any certitude. It is just speculation; so, beware.

Introduction

∼ ∼ ∼

When we look at the impact that knowledge of our own singular death has on our individual lives, we should recognize that it prompts responses. When we look at the impact knowledge of our death as a species has on our species, we should recognize that it prompts responses. These responses are our beliefs, stories, and actions that we build up to avoid the tragedy of our own mortality. Ernest Becker identified that "culture" is the development of our response to our death anxiety.

Becker has reported that when we develop cultural structures and paradigms (religious or social) they are all really getting at somehow building a layer between us and our fear of death. We are piling up all sorts of debris of belief to protect us from immediate contact with death itself. We are building a buffer zone.

In this view, we are always addressing the presence of our own death. We build it into everything we do. All of our movements in this life are to do some great thing that will preclude us from the common misery of death. In this instance, the Desert Fathers were not so much giving us a new commandment, but actually identifying a subconscious mechanism that exists in all of us. Everything we do is at some level a response to our death anxiety.

We remember our death so much that it drives us to do and be in different ways at every turn. Our living is nothing more than our preoccupation with our dying. Some of us are better at pretending this is not true or concealing the truth of this reality than others are.

What we may learn from Becker's foray into the desert arena of thinking is that we should pay attention to what we are doing in life because this will identify what we believe about death and how we are coping with our ensuing demise. Everything we do or say or hold within us reveals and betrays our response to our fear of death or what we can call the death anxiety.

In a society or country that is genuinely multi-cultural we have some complications surrounding this individual and social mechanism. If we are just simply one tribe, we develop one culture. This one culture is our agreed upon responses to our death anxiety—as a collective unit. It may or may not include a god or divine being, dances, medicine, songs, stories, diets, art, and other strata of praxis and dogma. We build a tower against our dying. The stronger and the higher the tower against death, the better we feel about ourselves and our one culture. It is the best; therefore. Our culture and our tower of belief is the best.

Now, add to that one culture and tribe, hundreds of other cultures and tribes. They are all living side by side. Some of the praxis and dogma that the cultures develop are in direct conflict and opposition to the praxis and dogma installed by other tribes in that same country or region. They are all the best (at least in their own estimations). They have all built towers of belief that are the best. In our linear world; however, not every one can be the best. There must be a BEST of the best.

This conflict necessitates either a battle to determine which culture is correct, or an isolation that simply ignores everything outside of its own beliefs and structures. There is yet a third response, and it is the response I believe we have struck on in our post-modern American society. This third response is to develop an overarching culture that trumps the lesser cultures and beliefs. We build a secret culture that we all really hold to; while still giving allegiance to our own one true culture.

We build a different tower of belief. This one we build with all of the other surrounding cultures. Then we can call that tower the BEST and we will still all be right by proximity and connection.

Now you get a hint of why people do not talk about death in a digital age. It is connected to our whole worldview and the stability or collapse of that worldview.

Out of Ernest Becker's theories developed a following. One particular approach to the issues that Becker analyzed comes from TMT or Terror Management Theory. This theory holds that our

Introduction

death anxiety causes enough of a cognitive dissonance in us that—as societies and as individuals—we build up buffers to the fear. In society we call these buffers cultures: religions, beliefs, groupings, clubs and the like. In individuals we call this buffer a sense of self-esteem or self worth.

In either category (societal or individual) we interpret people and groups that are contrary to our culture and our self-esteem as a threat to our stability. We tend to believe things that are different from us are wrong so we can bolster our own belief. "This is good; that is bad," is clearly one way we express this threat.

This theory is clearly worth looking into as the social scientists involved are highly credible individuals and have wonderful empirical findings to back up the theories. People fear death. Varying levels of that fear change who we are as individuals and as a people.

This will not be a linear discussion about death. This will be an amble, a wander, and a dance through, in and around all of the transformations in our life that we have shied away from. We will dance with death, we will dance with changes. Don't expect anything usual. Dance with me among the life that happens around the great transformation in dying into what comes next. Live with me for a while among the things that happen around the dying.

I will share some tales that come right from the bedside of the dying. These things happened around me while I held hands with dying people. They happened as I worked with uncovering the layers and layers of meaning behind peoples' fears and loves.

I will also share with you some of my own brushes with death. How has death impacted me? Where has he reared his head in my life? How have I gotten along amid that reality?

I will also drag out some tales from the ken of cultural development; things that cultures have said or expressed about death. How have artists have pictured death: painted it in word, canvas, or stone. I will also share a collection of poems about grieving, loss, and death.

Given that the world has become a single village (one that we are desperately trying to figure out) I would ask you to learn to suspend judgment and disbelief. Listen to the things that make us different. Do not simply brush away another persons beliefs or attempt at culture.

Remember, the one thing that we all are living toward and leaning into in this world—whether we are butcher, baker, candlestick maker, theologian, prostitute, congressman, or beggar—is that we are moving toward our death. Everything we do is somehow wrapped up, connected to, and impacted by that notion.

Wander with me, for a while if you will. You will never be the same. If any of these words that are gathered here can prod you into thinking about your own death and what you believe about it, and how that fits into other divergent belief, then I will have succeeded in what I had hoped to accomplish.

Chapter One

THE IDEA of death stalks us at every turn.

∼ ∼ ∼

It may actually be Death Himself that stalks us at every turn.

∼ ∼ ∼

Whether it is the idea of death or Death Himself, it does not matter. We are stalked throughout our whole lives by the notion, the idea, the feeling, the reality, and the imminent haunting dream that we are going to "not be alive" someday. Someday, what we are now will either not be at all or will somehow be different—very different. We are stalked by this at every turn.

I used to think that this was just something that I knew because of my work in hospice and my presence in the Orthodox Church.

In hospice all of my patients and their families were so surrounded by the issues of death and dying that Death was palpable. In the Orthodox Church the Fathers of the Church are still taught, and one of the main spiritual prescriptions of the Fathers was and is to "remember your death"—it will help you to live more soberly.

But, as I have moved away from these two magnets of death, I have begun to realize that Becker (Ernest Becker and his associates) were and are correct. All of us are at some semblance of odds with the idea of death and Death Himself. Everything we do has some foretaste of our "some-day-not-doing" or "some-day-not-being" mixed up in it. We are obsessed with the reality that we will not be around some day. It lies just below the surface of everything we do. It is an anxiety that we keep with us, allowing it to taint—ever so minutely—everything we are and do.

If you do not believe that, then just tear apart your motives for a whole day. Dissect them down to the drivers behind each thing you do. At some point you will be left with the idea that you do the things you do because either you believe they will put you into heaven (or hell) or that you do the things you do because you want to be a part of a group of people that are associated with that kind of behavior (which is also a way of painting an image of "heaven or hell"—it is your version of people doing the right thing and you do not want to be separated or isolated from that group).

I know it is easy to recoil from this bold idea and statement. None of us wants to think of ourselves or humanity as lemmings headed to the cliff; making turns this way and that to avoid the final frontier that will come to be regardless. But, as has become clearly the motto for our age, "it is what it is".

When we think about life, we think about belonging. We belong to a group or an ideal of what we think is the proper way. When we think about death, we think about being separated from our group or ideal—even if for an instant.

Death is that piece where we are "not-what-we-have-been". People of faith and religious leaning will probably balk at what I am saying—at first blush. But, an honest man/woman will recognize that his/her faith is faith because they want to stay connected to God (or the Divine Ideal) and God's community, even on the other side of the blinking instant of what we call death.

The reason the religious are religious is they do not want to be separated from this LIFE. They do not want to be separated from the TRUTH. Which is the premise that we are all doing what we do in life in response to the idea that we will not be alive some day.

This whole collection of words is about that idea. I am swimming in words about death and dying; about separation and belonging. This book is a wrestling with our wrestling with death. It is a sug-

Chapter One

gestion to look at how you wrestle with your fear of "not-being" and see how it impacts the way you live. It is a call to actively working with your own beliefs and a request to acknowledge your mythologies of death and dying.

Bring it up out of the unconscious and make it conscious. Because, as the Gospel of Thomas, 70 states so clearly: "If you bring forth what is within you, what you bring forth will save you. If you do not bring forth what is within you, what you do not bring forth will kill you."

Take a look at what is going on in yourself when you consider the idea of "not-being". What does it make you do, believe, feel, intuit, and desire? Remember your death—as the Fathers taught. It drives who you are. Be aware of that.

This one morning, I could feel Death's presence as I put on my socks. He was cold and heavy, sitting there without uttering a sound. He did not call to me, or draw a grasping hand at me. He just sat there. I could not even hear him breathe.

He lives on the back side of a fog we would do well to call ignorance. Sometimes we would do well to call the fog denial. Working with the dying has dissipated the fog some in my life. It is still there because so many people hide from the transformational ethos of dying, but I can see through it—like a haze—just a bit. The dying ones have made sure of that. They were eager to help me see.

It may not actually have been Death himself. It is hard to know if the presence you feel is Death or one of his minions (those that do His bidding). It is the same fine line between thinking about Death and thinking about dying. He and His minions have the same feel: cold and heavy, breathless. They are silent but clearly knowable. Talking about Death and dying has the same feel too. They are silencing. They bring an end to whatever is going on. Their lugubrious presence is heavy.

It felt like Death, though, this morning. Death sat there next to me on the bed. It sort of reminded me of the Looney Tunes cartoon when the sheep dog and the coyote go off to work together and punch in at the same time clock. Once they punch in, they become enemies, but before that they are just folks who know each other.

Death and I knew each other, but as I got closer to work—work at the hospice—He would become the very thing I was helping people to deal with. I would start to talk about Death like He was not there. He and I would be traveling together, but my job was to somehow open other peoples' eyes to His presence in their life, so they could be "awake".

You can tell when Death or His minions are in a room. You have been in a hospital room when nothing is being said, nothing is being felt. That not-saying and that not-feeling are because Death or His buddies are in the room—taking all of the life out of it. Death and his buddies consume everything—leaving a vacuous void. Silence beyond anything we could give word to.

If you are not sure of what I am talking about, just say the word "death" the next time you are talking with a group of people. Simply interject the word into the middle of the conversation—an absurd non-sequitur.

The blank, expressionless absence of words that saying "death" creates, that feeling is the feeling of Death himself. He has gained that feeling because we have filled his image with elemental impressions that are filled with fear. Our innards writhe at the mention of the word. The anxiety that swims in us is an overbearing pile of snakes. They steal our tongue and dull our minds. Just utter the word, you will see.

He is what we have created him to be. Not that Death does not have his own intrinsic meaning. It does. He does. But, impressions add to meaning—that is for sure. Fear has added an immense stock of impressions to what is conjured up when we hear the mention of "Death" or think in his direction.

When we do not talk about something, we are not saying that there is no belief behind that idea; that we have nothing inside us concerning that thing. We are saying that we struggle with being able to put words to what it is that is going on inside. This is what the Gospel of Thomas, 70 was getting at. If we do not put words to that thing in us, it will consume the whole of our days and drive us toward its own self fulfillment. Basic psychology, folks.

We can have all sorts of linear beliefs about death and dying; "bumper sticker phrases" to shield our hearts from the dread we feel. But, most people when faced with transformation are not permeated with a peaceful surrender that longs for transition. They recoil with some ancient lurking sickness that is beyond them. Their dark silence runs deep. We fear Death most often.

His minions are made up of the recently dead, and His spiritual envoys—angels of Death if you will. His minions are new arrivals and the long-dead alike. His minions do his bidding. They are journeymen and masters. His minions are also small thoughts, images, and inklings of the idea of separation, loss, and death. Little things that give us a glimpse—askance—of death.

You could say there are layers to the impressions and meaning of Death. There are pieces to the complete identity of Death. They float aloft like wisps of carbon around a fire. Those layers, those pieces, and those wisps make up the minions of Death.

Most of the time people do not recognize that things in our lives have multiple and graded meanings. They do not recognize the layers to things. They believe they have streamlined and singular beliefs about things like God and love and death and sex.

The fact is, most of us have concentric meanings and impressions about everything in our world. Without them we would be unable to survive. The echolocation of our lives is always seeking out where things are in conjunction to where we are. This sensing is able to identify depth where we had only thought there was a surface. We just do not rely on this sensing; we do not feel for more than initial soundings.

When you feel Death, it may be a minion. It may just be one of the recent dead who are unfamiliar with what has happened to them. It may be remnants of a conversation on the dismal topic. It may be Death himself has perched himself aloft in the space around you. It may simply be lineaments of your last funeral. You can feel Death, though. You can feel the presence of the idea of dying. It may be a missing of someone you no longer have within view; just outside your reach, and touch, and grasp.

When people die, some of them do not die knowing they are dying. Quick and sudden deaths are like this. These people seek out the living in order to carry on usual relationships with them. Since they do not know they are dead, they do not know they should stop living—and so they do not. They just keep on carrying on with "life" as they knew it. All the while, they are dead. Their echolocation is really poorly developed. It can happen with people that are in deep concentric rings of denial or ignorance—those who have not allowed things to come up and out into the conscious light.

These unclear dead folks—transformed people who do not know they are transformed—try to crash in to familiar scenes. They go down the hall from their death room and seek out urgent and familiar feelings. They look for "Clara" or "Bob" and launch off into some one-sided, unheard conversation.

They run after their sister that is running out of the house in tears. The gap between living and dying is not as cavernous as we had hoped. We see people who have died for weeks after the change has happened.

Chapter One

The newly dead try to meet up with people. They are trying to see if things are really as different as they feel, or if they are only exaggerating what they feel. It is sort of like walking into a meeting and immediately joining into the conversation. You kind of hope people will forget you were late. That is what the newly dead do, if they did not know Death was coming. They are hoping people will somehow forget they are late. They are a bit unsure of their own lateness as well.

It is amazing to me that more of them do not recognize something is odd right at the outset. But, for many it takes a while to orient their new world with the old world. Gibran was right: death is sort of like a denied poet or prophet. It is in our midst, but we have not ears to hear or eyes to see.

After a while, the newly dead begin to sense that something is different. At first, there is no real knowing, but there is a sensing that things are not the same. The "knowing" that they are dead, comes later. It happens when they meet another transformed person who comes to help, or it comes when they have attempted to talk to the living so many times that they can piece together why they fail to respond.

The living go through this same shift. We often see those who have died. They are just across the room. We see them at a distance in the mall. We are sure that they were in that meeting. We will eventually stop seeing the dead in our homes, and malls, and lives as well. We will get on with life and our minds will adjust. We tell ourselves it is over and they are gone. But the gap is not as cavernous as we had hoped.

We all have a period of adjustment to go through when death occurs. The living as well as the dead.

I have had patients meet up with me in my home. They are looking for someone they can openly confide in. They all live at least forty minutes away from me, and have no idea where I live, but they show up, wanting to connect. I mean dead ones meet me. The impressions of these patients meet me; their spirits meet me; the essence of who they are meets me. The newly dead seek out the familiar and will go at great lengths to feel comfortably familiar with their new life. And so, those who need me to help make sense out of what is going on have met up with me. If only in a dream.

I am not sure if this is a violation of patient privacy, other newly dead meeting me and seeding themselves into where I am going? But, at any rate, HIPAA violation or not, they seek out life because they don't know it is missing. They follow me into my day. They hope I will not notice that they have shown up to the meeting late.

There was one MHMR patient I had visited for months while she was alive. She was—at first—unsure of why we were meeting, even though we were speaking about being sick and about death. Her parents would not allow any of us on the hospice staff to make the connection with her predicament and her dying. We could not talk about her death. I spoke about it tangentially for months.

I spoke about it tangentially because I believe that is all that is necessary for people to do the work themselves and make the inner connection. She did. Against her parents wishes she brought forth that which was within.

She showed up at my house one morning at two o'clock. She marched into my dream and waking all at once. She suddenly knew she was dying and her vaporous self tracked me down. She said to me, "I don't know how to do this." She wanted my help.

I explained it to her. I talked about transitions. I sat down, felt around my heart for an idea of what she was going through. When I felt/saw the scenario, I explained her way through it. I told her how to travel through the landscape of her dying.

When she arrived in my dream, I could smell her presence in my waking. It was the smell some dying people have mixed with her household odors. The smell was so strong that I knew she was coming to me before she actually appeared. I could smell her; in

Chapter One

my sleeping and in my waking. I knew her in the shadows. The smell made my dream turn to lucidity.

We encounter these shadows in the land between waking and sleeping. We encounter the deeper mysteries in the lingering awareness that lacks domination by control: in the land of words and images, impressions and hunches. We can see and hear these things when we loosen our grip just a little bit. This ties dreaming to our wakefulness; dreaming is a part of the process of bringing forth that which is within to save us.

She was genuinely scared. She had no idea what to do. She remembered that I had told her if she had questions about what was happening, or needed help, that she should ask me. I would be honored and glad to help.

I felt into my heart to find out where we were; where she was. There had been a clear and deep-sapphire blue tunnel in front of us—as I felt around for impressions. From the center of the tunnel came a rich and scintillating gold light. It was so rich and dense; it looked like flowing or churning liquid gold. I knew this place well. It was the place people go to in meditation. I had been there before. It was then I realized that meditation builds a bridge to transformation.

The inner journey is a mirror of the outer. Meditation is tied to death. Meditation is tied to surrendering into the letting go that is death.

I told her about what I saw and told her that it was a good sign. It was the sign of peace and the unitive experience—good will and harmony. I told her people had sought this vision of God for thousands of years. Mystics strove to find this place. She had arrived at the Divine source and would be able to go on ahead. She had found the Pearl of Great Price.

She said she was scared. I told her how I had been at this place hundreds of times and it was a good place. This place was exactly where she needed to be. I assured her that the beauty of everything she saw around her was an important thing for her to focus on and concentrate on. She could trust this place.

She said she trusted me, and she would just look at the beauty of it all. I told her to go into the tunnel and enjoy her time there, that there would be friends for her to see. She left and went on her way. She trusted what we saw together, and that my having been there before was enough. She not only brought forth what was within, but she then entered into it.

When she was gone, the smell that had filled the room slowly disappeared as well. The smell was the distinct odor of dying, of household cleaners used to rid the home of the smell of death, and of cigarette smoke that had filled her home her last few months of life. It was in both the dream and in my waking nostrils. It faded after a few minutes of being awake.

It was gone. When I got to work that morning, I found out she had died in the early morning hours. I already knew that.

She must have been lonely, needed some more help—on the other side, or getting there—or been missed deeply. Two weeks after her death, her mother died—unexpectedly. I like to believe she took the journey for her daughter; she longed to go it together. Perhaps the reason the parents did not want to speak to the daughter about death was because the mother had sensed her own imminent demise. Who can say?

Sometimes when you feel the numbing presence of death it is one of Death's spirits or angels coming to lure you onto the path. They don't have any ability to bring you onto the path; they just randomly attempt to catch unsuspecting and weak victims. They hope you lose your focus just enough to steer off the road, or slip with the chainsaw. They hope they can surprise you into dying. Every close call you have had where you emerge knowing you almost died is a clear example. It may be that the minions have a bonus program for bringing in new members. If you have a sudden and traumatic end, they get a toaster or a sandwich grill. Who can say?

Chapter One

I was no fool. I wasn't going that morning—that morning that I felt Death's presence. I was not going to follow Him or them into my own death. But, I would certainly walk with them and find out who was getting ready to take the path. I would put on my socks and go off with Death to minister among the dying.

Working with the dying is like being in the underworld. It is all misty and hazy and you are not sure about what you are seeing or hearing. But, you learn to work with a deeper sense—intuition and discernment. You learn to listen for things, feel for things, look, taste, and touch for things with a more hyper-extended sense of understanding.

Like in dreams and dreamtime things in the luminal and liminal world of the dying are very metaphoric and operate on a vast array of planes of meaning and action. One thing means more than one thing. This is always an important distinction when applying therapeutic skill toward interpreting a life lived.

This same sort of dreamtime or dreamlike living occurs in leaping poetry. The connections made between disparate ideas, concepts, and objects in this kind of poetry are not only metaphoric, but able to span the full range of the synapses in the brain. Things may not immediately make sense in proximity to each other, but then, all of the sudden, the link is illuminated and we have an "ah ha moment" that makes everything liminal and luminal at once. It is dreamy.

Things that do not seem to be connected, related, or meaningful together become so because of the awakening moment. End-of-life has a lot of these awakening moments. These same sort of things happen quite frequently in meditative or contemplative states and experiences. We are opened to a much wider field of interpretation and awareness. We can see how one thing may be related to, similar to , or connected to another in this arena of "larger meaning". This gives it an underworld or subconscious feel.

DANSE MACABRE

People in the end-stage-of-life, and to an extent the people immediately around them, are forced into seeing through the looking glass with a bit more intensity than every other day in life. The best we can do to describe it is to compare it to those really serious conversations, thoughts, and pacts that come about in the evening as the sun is setting. You know those serious conversations that happen around the fire, or heart to heart, or over a glass of wine. Everything else in life—except that moment—is meaningless. This conversation bears the weight of our whole worth and of the whole world.

Things are so different in this liminal and luminal space that often the morning after one of these serious and clarifying moments, people tend to down play how vital those conversations, thoughts, or pacts were. They may even deny that they said this or that. You know what I am talking about. That is how it is all of the time in the lives of people edging closer to death. Everything is vital and means something. More of life leans into the liminal and luminal as death approaches.

I know this language sounds silly to you. But, play along; the journey we shall take will bridge the gap between your fear and your living. Hold the words and let them ring aloud a bit. Find out where the words belong and where you are in relation to them.

Without these impressions, you will hold the images below the luminal life and keep them at bay for ever. That will kill you. Let these tales become the solid matter in the field of your echolocation. They will give resonance to your soundings.

Someday—generally sooner than we hope—Death will come for you. Can you honestly say that at this moment now you feel ready to make the transition? Is everything in your life in order and up to date? Have you mended everything that is torn? Have you added everything you were here to add? If not, dance with me among the stories of Death and dying and find some flowers to hold onto for beauty and sustenance against the change.

Chapter One

Who was there that morning—the morning I was putting on my socks—I do not know. I do know that one of the Death squad was there. I could feel them: heavy and lingering like that fog. They wanted something. I had no idea what it was. I could feel they wanted something.

I had put my socks on inside out. I had to take them off and turn them "right side out" (the lumps of loose string facing thread in) and put them back on. This focus; this "little-extra-to-get-it-right" time with my socks gave me the chance to step out of the routine and feel him there. He was close: very, very close. Small acts of routine behavior are often the bridges into contemplative space. Somehow the repetitive nature of routine enables us to step off the bridge and into the Stream-of Life. Routine can plunge us into the underworld—the world of "that which is within".

Routine helps us to step outside of ourselves and notice things like this. Things like the presence of Death. Things like how much we love the people in our lives. I let the routine reveal to me the path of my day. Someone was dying and I would be needed sooner, rather than later.

My pager went off. When I returned the page, the nurse told what house to go to. That is where I went.

Chapter Two

The Medieval paintings, and drawings, and woodcuts that depict skeletons rising from their graves and tempting the living to join them in "The Danse Macabre", are not far off. They are not wrong. There is a clear reality that hangs on them like those wisps of smoke—like that carbon around the fire. Those images are clothed with hand-me-downs of the truth.

The macabre dance of the dead is something that goes on all around us. The living and the dead are always interacting. It is happening at the level of muons and quarks. Everything is in a transition from one state to another. Everything. We call it growth. The cosmos is bursting with things that are, things that have been, and things that will be. They are all always in relation to one another.

The freshly dead, the wandering dead, and the spirit-angels of Death himself all try to entice us to follow them. They are lonely. They want company. They need to create a reality that is communal. Without a community, they would feel dead and alone. That would be too much for them to bear. So, they mingle with us looking for companionship. They want us to join their reality. They need something we have.

We are pulled and pushed into growth and evolution by the play of energies and forces. The negative charge draws a positive charge. Things diminish to emerge renewed. Living begets dying and dying begets living in everything.

It is richer than this. Endings are everywhere around us. We are becoming adults and dying to our youth. We are becoming single and dying to our marriages. We are changing jobs and dying to our vocations. We are deepening in our understanding and dying to our ignorance. We go to sleep and wake up; we wake up and go to sleep. We remember; we forget. We are all always engaged in a process of dealing with life and death. That is the Danse Macabre.

Just as we are finding out in the New Physics, one event in our lives exists at the same time as all the other events in our lives. The thing we call time and the thing we call space are not as concrete as we had earlier depicted them—or, perhaps as we had hoped. There is more of an exchange between local and non-local events. There are wormholes and black holes in space, time, and in a human life as well.

Dying and death are whirling about us in a cosmic motion. One thing is transforming into another every second of time throughout all time. This is part of the macabre dance. This becomes that, and that becomes this. Cutting the atom of all life has revealed a massive force and dynamism behind everything. One thing is always dying into another—transforming into newness. We are no different.

Countless Classical authors wrote about these happenings, this dance under the titles of "The Nature of Things". They tried to put the pieces together in everything that was. Contemporary scientists resurrected the idea when they began to search for the unified theory of everything. That theory would be one that would isolate and identify how each and everything fits into the whole of this thing we call life. The dance of life is also the dance of death.

When we start to tell the tales about Death and when we start to tell the tales about the nature of things we are weaving our own tapestry of myths. The stories are coming up and out of us; dancing if you will.

What makes myth so critical in the life of a human is not its simple ability to calm and soothe us—stories do tend to deescalate the anxieties in us and calm us down. What makes myth so critical is how it enhances our word power—it helps us merge the two hemispheres of our brain.

The stories, the dramas, and the archetypes of mythology shape and deepen our word power. People with a fuller and more comprehensive word power have a broader field of resources from which to choose and shape their outcomes and responses in life as well as their interpretation of these outcomes. People with a larger word power tend to feel they have more options. This is no accident.

Myth and the subsequent stories, dramas, and archetypes that go along with myth demand that we place words in certain order so we can tell the tales that myths represent. The way we use and place words, enhances the depth of meaning that those words are able to portray and relate. The more meaning words have, the more options people have.

What is going on as words deepen in meaning is that we are using more of our brain in the process. When we enter into myth, we are entering into same role and function that dreams, poetry, and imagination play in the life of the human. They unite both the left and right hemispheres of the brain. Thinking and feeling merge and we stand on the apex of brain function. The brain not only thinks and stores, it intuits and feels, but only through its neurological linkage with the rest of the body.

Increased word power is increased ability to unite the features found within the human species. Without these abilities, we are less than we could be. Myth plays a critical role in human development.

This is the reason that the dying see people and places that are meaningful to them. The words (in this case the images of people and places) that have become the most meaningful to them in life—that have carved the deepest cavern of meaning in them—are what is most important to them. As they lay on their death bed, only the things that are most important to them will stay with them the closer they get to dying.

I have seen this over and over again. The lesson from this is that the words, stories, images, dramas (or the MYTHS) that we allow to carve the deepest meanings in our lives—the things we assign the most important meaning to—these things will be what we are surrounded by at death. What will surround you at death? What myths have you invested with ultimate and deep meaning? Do you really want to see those at the end?

The most prevalent mythology in this current day and age—in almost all societies—is a mythology based on and steeped in both technology and consumerism. The stories and tales we tell, the dramas and archetypes we reenact on a daily basis are all about technology and consumerism. We spend so much of our culture making and family making time trying to get a hold of the latest thing and the latest gadget so we can stay ahead of the "trend" curve.

This means that the stories we would tell around the fire would be less about the origin of the universe, the cosmos, and our species, and more about our conquests in the mall. And, although conquest stories have always been told around the fire (in the form of stories of war and battle), these conquests are not about how we did what we did to protect our clan or village. All the stories are about individual conquests to make us as individuals look better. These are not good society building myths.

I would venture a guess that these two myths have become part of our human hopes and desires. We long to attain to a higher level of technology and consumerism. We hunger after individual gain of "stuff". Oh that we would hunger for individual gain of beauty, truth, or goodness. Oh that we would consume the traits of wisdom, patience, and compassion. Stuff and gadgets do not carry the same glory. In my view.

If this is so, we have supplanted some very deep and rich human aspirations. We may be seeing the tail end of a fuller and more comprehensive expansion of word power. People may have traded imagination for gadgets and stuff. If that is the case, we are in trouble.

In a world that has made technology and consumerism its central myth, who shows up for you at the death bed? Do we imagine we see our iPad or our credit card come to see us off into the next world? Will our smart phone or our hybrid be at the other end of the great tunnel of light?

Only Death himself can effectively put you on the trail to dying. These messengers will not be the ones who initiate us into the great change. They are just a distraction toward our fears. Death is the tipping point toward transformation. It is his dharma; it is his karma; it is his job. Death is the forerunner of new life. So, we had better get better at talking about it; especially since everyone wants new life and new growth.

There are others like Death—there are smaller deaths. There are daily episodes that remind us of the process: like sleeping and waking that we spoke about before. They are samples of the big death. If we would pay attention we would know that. Rumi was clear about it when he said: "What have I ever lost by dying." Every dream of letting go has assured you of the same. Losing a job or a certain way of life is a death as well; a little death, but a death.

We need to weave ourselves between words about Death (the Big DEATH of the body) and words about the shifts (the little deaths of life's process) if we expect to make any headway in understanding this deep mystery. We need to see the microcosm in the macrocosm. It is a way of bringing the sublimated conversation into liminal and luminal space. We pull the discussion up out of repression when we can connect the impressions between one transformation and all transformations. When we see how small deaths mimic the big death.

If you ever want to stop fearing Death, you had better begin to see it as one with all transformations. There is only one escape and that is surrender.

Make friends with your dying. Or as the mystics have always taught: "Die before you die". All of these little deaths and big deaths fit into the macabre dance. They fit into the dance of life. So, grab the hand of your past, your present and your future.

Chapter Two

Your life is a part of the universal life dance. You are in the DNA of the unified theory of everything. You are a part of the dance, whether you bring that forth from within yourself or not. It would fit into a theory of an elegant and unified universe (theory of everything), or a true and beautiful universe that everything is in relation to everything else that is—whether it is or is not conscious of it's fitting in.

So, whether you say the goal is to bring forth that which is within, or the goal is to see how you fit into the cosmic dance it does not matter. Being awake is the goal. Being aware is the prize. The reality of things being in relationship to each other will go on and on and on whether you are aware of it or not. Being aware then becomes the prize. It is the "pearl of great price". Everything else is an image.

I am pretty sure people will always fear death. It is something that we will always need to instruct toward healing. Most people will not arrive at the clear-sighted and pragmatic wisdom of Rumi. Rumi said, "What have I ever lost by dying." He made this statement in one of his stanzas. The preceding lines were about having been a rock and then a plant and then an animal and then a human. In all of the dying and being born-again, he never felt he lost out in the deal.

You do not have to lean into a belief of reincarnation to have the same fragrance of dispassion ("apatheia" in classical theology). You can genuinely arrive at this same conclusion when you look back over a life lived and notice that you have survived through countless little-death experiences. You emerge—eventually—from all of the chaos and confusion. The Anglo-Saxon's used to say, "That evil ended. So also, shall this." This just simply gets at the notion that each individual event in life is a part of some larger thing. The aggregate is not the whole. And, the little parts and pieces of life are always moving. Some days you have bad experiences; some days you have good ones. Some days you have a blend of both.

DANSE MACABRE

When we are detached from the cycle of birth and death that exists in nature we are more inclined to fear death. Our fear comes from an existential dread that is tied to falling out of rhythm with the cycles of life. When you live in the wild, there is a fuller connection with birth, sickness, suffering, and death. When you plant the fields and harvest the fruit, you tend to get the idea of the cycle. You cannot escape it. There is always a deer carcass to move, an injured bird to tend, trees to cut, seeds to harvest and plant, and compost to spread.

You take things to the earth to break them down. Life comes out of dead things. Living and dying are a part of the dance.

The advent of ever sprawling cities has changed the visage of our belief. We are no longer surrounded by the great earth that turns all things to dirt. We are surrounded by macadam. Dead things on macadam do not fall apart the same way they do on dirt. I think this makes us see "things-falling-apart" as unnatural. In the woods and on the farm, dead things tend to merge into the dirt. In the city, they tend to pile up.

You can stretch this image too far, and it will be useless, but at its root it is good common sense. Where you have room to live on the earth and see its ongoing and relentless cycles, you are more inclined to see death and dying as a natural part of the process of life. Where you do not have that room to live and see, you feel for different rhythms—different cycles. The natural world does not allow us to push the reality down inside without bringing it forth first.

Once we bring forth the matter that lies in that great Underground River of the Self we then begin to see that its releases are similar, but different for each release by other individual selves. The great unconscious slightly alters the released images based on culture, experience, and vantage point.

The prescription of the Gospel of Thomas—to find our salvation by letting things out of the well—is only the beginning of the Gordian knot that we must untangle. The prescription of the Fathers'—to remember our death—is only the beginning of the journey toward being awake. They are the singular pieces that break through our dualistic thinking and help us to find Heidegger's "deep thinking" or Krishnamurti's "truth". They are the silent opening into being that emerges only after the koan is pondered a thousand lifetimes. They push and pull us into the great underground river. They are the alluring start to something large. They are a siren's call into the water.

Before the Divisions

Go back to the place
you were before you
gathered images and inklings.

Return to the you
that was before
the divisions
of learning took place.

Enter the underground stream
from which everything
flows into separateness

but do not
come back.

Once you stop swimming
between the two worlds
and just let go,
you will have brought the two
together as one.

DANSE MACABRE

Once you allow
that which is within you
to come out and save you,

quick, jump in
and drown in the oneness.

That will be your
awakening. On that day
you will have been
born again.

Chapter Three

Peoples' fears of death will shift and change through life, as well. When we are younger we tend to be brash and cool. Death is nothing to us. But, as the list of the dead increases in our memories; and as the number of dead peers rises, we encounter a seasoned change that betrays wear and tear.

When we are young death is possible but unlikely. As we age, death becomes not only possible, but also likely. It takes a lot to stave that off that for very long.

Just like the concentric rings and layers behind things, we see that the DNA of our own place in the dance is made up of small little dances on how we look at and interact with death throughout the stages of our lives. Like little side ambles or waltzes, we find that death means one thing to us in childhood, but another thing in old age. We twist and turn and twirl through our dance, altering the steps as we go. We find we are changing and developing through time and space: dancing.

When we are young we may fear dying old and decrepit. We want there to be some sort of deathbed realization and victory, so we find ourselves lost in myths of Constantine's deathbed baptism or the chivalric knight running in at the last moment to save the dire situation for the damsel in distress. Our youthful mythologies are filled with black and white forces doing battle and being saved from one another.

These myths lose their appeal as we age and begin to feel the ailing loss of power and energy in life and limb. We turn more toward myths of slipping into death like drifting off into sleep. Or we hold high the need to see our dead relatives as we wander aimlessly across the river Styx. There seems to be a diminishment of startling and polarized images of life as we age. Our images begin to replicate the compromise we are living into in our midlife.

Young people tend to love to do battle. By the time we hit mid-life we have seen enough battling and realize that neither side really wins. Rights and wrongs lose their way to peace and harmony. At first we compromise and then we stop looking for ways to win anything at all. That quiescence toward surrender is a sign of wisdom, not simply years. It is a realistic look at years of reviewing our outcomes. We stop pandering to hope and tend to accept the brittle notion that we will not always win.

I was really not prepared for the small death of having my sons not need me any longer. Well, not entirely, but you know what I mean.

I believed and still do in offering them all of the tools they need to grow and thrive and make their way in the world. So, I should be happy that as they entered teenage years they were thriving individuals—capable and unique. They want and are able to be men.

Somewhere in their growing up; somehow in their individuation my heart became attached to loving them and my soul began to thrive on nurturing them. Around the same time my mind apparently stopped remembering that this was a biological function happening here—one that had an expiration date on it. Someday they would not need this lifeline. Someday they would be tall enough to look me in the eye and be my equal; able to gather the things they need to survive; all by themselves.

And so, as the day began to approach my inner knowing longed for what used to be. I began to miss the little sons that they had been—the ones with craft projects and scraped knees. I wished I was needed to read a bedtime story, to sing a goodnight song, or to spin a yarn about a childhood memory of mine that was similar to something they were doing.

Chapter Three

It has never quelled my preparing them to be men. We spend a lot of time talking about options for ways to respond to situations and examples of how to be as an individual adult male. But, my heart wants them to be talking with me about fishing and dragons, trolls and building forts. Alas.

It would be nice to receive some sort of "credit" for having gone through this stage as a young man—you know; I went through this as a young man so I am prepared for going through it as a dad. The truth is, even though we have been through these changes from the "other-side" or the "other perspective" it does nothing to prepare us for what we will go through when our young mature and leave home. We will only know a bit of what they are feeling and going through because we have gone through it. Even that will be a shadow compared to their own individual and unique experience.

These shifts happen regularly. They happen in every area of our lives. They happen in each and every phase and stage of what it means to be human.

Marriage has these same shifts. After that first year you start to get a taste for the deep intimacy and resolution that is going to be needed if two people are going to co-habitate and forge a life for themselves together. Before that, a lot of life can be hormonal drives to mate and procreate; keeping us blind to the things that truly separate and make us unique. Inevitably, like some ancient interior time clock, there is a day you wake up and realize that the other person is way different than you. It is as if the shear animal attraction floods your system and clouds your perception to things that you would normally be alarmed at. It is not horrible, just different.

A lot of people never get beyond this dying shift in marriage to be able to learn to accept and integrate "the other" into their own unique life. This stage is critical if you are going to have kids. It becomes the relationship within which you get to practice coming to terms with our opposites. You begin to experience riding through the waves of variety, difference, and separateness.

A lot of folks never learn this rhythm and find comfort only in those pieces of relationships where they feel at one with the other; connected and always in unison. Instead of living through the dying and rebirth of the relationship into new stages and phases, they just simply let that relationship die and then the start a new one hoping to find all of the missing pieces from the first one. Either way; dying and rebirth is a cycle we will never escape.

These pieces of the relationship will die and be reborn over the years. Some years (as one of my hospice patients so aptly proclaimed) are better than others; some years are great. Practicing dying and being reborn in these relationships will eventually give you the tenacity to get through the tough stuff that will inevitably come at you by virtue of being alive.

Living and dying gives you a skin.

I have noticed the cycle of life and death in jobs and vocations as well. Aside from the rhythmic ups and downs that go along with careers, there are also outright changes of jobs and changes of direction. Sometimes you wake up and wonder who put you on this road. Other times, you are content to wander and journey on the road you are on.

All of these situational developments, these changes in the way things are, these shifts in being are a part of the overall image of death in our lives. When one thing becomes another, when one thing ceases to be, when we move beyond what we know reality to be at this moment we experience a death. Each one is new. And, while practice makes you better at it, part of the uniqueness of each event is that it will hold a bit of a different taste or flavor. Each death, though categorically similar will ask for different things from us.

This sense of uniqueness of experience takes time to get used to.

Chapter Four

THE IMAGES of the dance of death did not just inhabit the consciousness of medieval survivors of the plague. These were images that someone grabbed a hold of from a larger ken. They were and still are an en-fleshing of an archetype—a reality that we sense and feel but cannot necessarily see or hear. They have been around long before the rats and fleas carried the plague of bubons through Europe.

This reality has existed from the moment conscious life stirred itself into knowing. It is the same archetype that allows an Einstein to decide that there is some theory out there (some unified dance) that expresses the unified nature of all that is. The unified theory of everything is the dance of death, the dance of life.

One being that has died—one thing that has become transformed—longs for companionship. The dead want friends. Flowers want a bunch. The movement of life itself is to push ahead and replicate itself.

So, a dandelion changes from being one into being many by changing from a flower into seeds. A body becomes a part of the many by seeding itself in transformation. Caught on the wind of life's motion, it is planted in the luminal world of numinosity. It can only be planted by dying into a seeded existence.

Everything is swirling in a rhythmic relationship, moving in and out of relations with everything else that exists. A dead salamander rots and becomes the dirt that will grow a trout lily. A phase in our lives disappears only to be the groundwork for some later passage we must make.

DANSE MACABRE

This powerful and almost erotic teasing of life to be passed on is exactly at the root of the image of the skeleton motioning us to join the dance of death and pass on. "Come and be with me, come and keep me company. Come and dance with me."

The image gets at the notion of companionship on the singular journey. Birth and death are both singular journeys. We make them by ourselves. The Dance of Death ties the reality of death to community so people don't feel alone or abandoned when confronting the notion of death.

This enticing call is probably the only way to get people to go. If you cannot allure them into the journey, they would not naturally make the choice to die. It is a wonderful archetypal myth and image from within our depths. Bring it forth and it will save you. Leave it in there and it will kill you.

It is almost as if the biology of the movement within our body—the flow of blood, and food, and bile through our multiple systems within—is demanding we tell stories to replicate its reality. It is as if the cells inside want us to tell their tale. Our myths echo what we cannot see.

The Danse Macabre paints a scene of camaraderie along a road too bleak to journey alone. The images of our mythologies are meant to be pictures, and sounds that set us free from fear: hollers into the dark. They are meant to portray the jolly nature that Death tries to present to us so we will follow along. They are stories and myths trying to help us cognitively yield to the notion of death.

The gut knows we must die. Even the heart knows we must die. The mind likes to think we can avoid it. The mind is a city-dweller.

If we have no stories about death or no words about dying then we have only fear at the unknown. Our modern age has traded most of its stories, images, sights and sounds for anxiety and fear. Stop talking and the silence echoes into a deafening existential dread. That is what has become of death. Say the word aloud. I dare you. Say it in a crowd. See what happens.

Chapter Four

But, this is a path we would do well to learn to tread. We would do well to start telling tales. They will be weak at first, but get over it. They will become better as we learn the telling.

When we are in the presence of the singular nature of life we are meant to gather and collect "more-ness" and others all about us. Pulling at sympathetic union like the collapsing of gases in a star that is about to rebound into a super nova rebirth; we explode out of solitary existence into the unified field of everything.

Death is not an end. Nature knows no end. Neither does God. We need to bring that up and out of us. If we shove it back down in, then we are proclaiming that there is an end and that will kill us, ultimately. Tell the tales of Death's transforming nature.

Just like our birth into the community of the living, the Danse Macabre archetype is a bridge for us to be born into the community of the dead. Being completely alone is an idea we shrink from. It is better to be able to expect moments of togetherness. Life is not singular, but plural.

So, these medieval paintings and carvings were a way of talking about the idea of death and about death itself. They were a way of taking the inner fears of isolation and turning them into communal experiences of unification. They were a telling of the stuff that was within us. They would unite living and dying together.

Danse Macabre images made a chorus out of what we had considered a solo-performance. We have lost our communal pageants. We have lost our corporate dramas. Bring up your images, fears, and inklings about death. They will only unite you with the other living members of the unified field of everything. Push them back down in and below the surface of your consciousness and you will only be denying the reality of life itself.

How we speak of death will reveal what we believe about our lives. Is it a normal and usual transformational movement among the patterns of life? Does it bring us into communion with the "Other/others"? Does it assign us to singular condemnation and suffering?

DANSE MACABRE

How you speak about death is how you speak about life and living into it. Ultimately it is tied to your pictures and words about God. Tread lightly, but tread with interest.

Our living is tied together with our dying. The dead are all about the living; if not in spiritual space, then in memory. We see it at the end-of-life all of the time.

Dying people see dead aunts and uncles and friends and loved ones coming to collect them; to take them over to the other side. They transform from one state into another and gather the things they need to make the change.

The two things we would like to be able to clearly separate and define as separate are intricately woven together. Death and life are somehow connected; somehow one. It is as if relatives and loved ones come to demand from you that you pay attention to what is happening—that you look at what is going on and do not shove it back down inside. Wake up, do not deny reality.

However you grab at this myth of death, the idea is that Death is around us—all of the time. Some cannot accept the idea of an embodied character, and so for them it is ideal to state that the possibility of death is always present. But, others know Death as a being, and know him to be always at hand—himself or his cronies.

However you talk about Death—as an imagistic being or simply a state—it/He is most intimately conjoined with life. How do you interpret the image of the dance of death and the dance of life? How do you piece together the living and the dead? What is your myth about the unified theory of everything? If you do not acknowledge this union, you will clearly be afraid.

What if we thought of life as a game of tag? What if instead of ignoring or sublimating the idea that things stop being one way and are transformed into another way, we just believed that things are always shifting? Things go from being IT (as in tag), to being NOT IT. Life is a dance of one form becoming another. Moving in and out of relation to everything that is, we are dancing through

Chapter Four

the unified field of all that is. Time and space are not limitations, simply the path we tread—the steps we take.

You do not need to leave out an idea of the Divine. How is it that the Holy One—blessed be He—is involved in this ongoing set of changes?

Chapter Five

WE ARE at a loss in our nation. We have wiped out, or at least weakened the images of Death in our respective cultural mythologies. He is very weak in our mythologies because of our cultural plurality and diversity. Most myths are weak in our lives because if we tell them at all we whisper them.

Living in this digital age where the importance of nationality, culture, and distinction has been replaced with speed, information, and flexibility has had an impact on our human mechanisms—our interior mechanisms. It is wonderful for industry and technology, but these are not necessarily the healthiest of human attributes.

Our myths are weak because we have believed that the response to standing amid multi-cultural representations of interior myths is to throw them all away as irrelevant and become "modern". We somehow tell ourselves that because the story is being told differently by other people, that perhaps there is no truth to any of the tales. We forget that the underlying fact that we make myths is perhaps the truth that is trying to be told. It is not the how or why or when that the myths are all about. They are about the fact that making myths is vital.

In this case many people have "trashed" their individual cultural systems of belief—stating that they are arcane or outdated. They have sought to modernize their way of life; which they believe means laying aside anything that their parents and grandparents held as vital. They dismiss this layer of their lives as superstitious.

Perhaps our myths are weak because we see all the divergent cultural myths that exist and think that they are useless since there are so many—fearing that we need to make a decision about which

Chapter Five

one is most worthwhile or most true. This is not the case. We can live amid many diverse and even conflicting ideas, beliefs, and myths (look at the Classical mythologies or African and Norse mythologies) without having to punish, evaluate, or reward one over the other. It is difficult, but not impossible.

There are so many diverse and rich myths about death because myths work their magic in individuals as well as in cultures. Each culture has its own "stuff" it needs to allow to come up and out of its "self" and each individual within that culture has the same. The stuff that comes up and out will be just a bit different from others'. It will have chips and pieces of individual experience blended into its telling.

The shifts that come from individual belief within a culture are no different that the shifts that come from multicultural beliefs within a society or nation. There will be and must be more than one. The little nuances of difference are shaping depth and character in the tellings. They add to believe-ability.

If we have learned anything from the "Arab Spring" that is moving across the globe in this spring and summer of 2011, it is that people that have been repressed and hopes that have been repressed hunger and long to be set free. When that hungering and longing reaches a critical mass, it will rise up and out. The uprisings all across the Middle East have been about people wanting a voice. The world is poised not simply to accept "democracy"—a political system. The world is poised to accept multiculturalism and tolerance as well. These are not always inclusive issues. Some are more relevant for people who have been repressed; some are more immediately needed.

Just like an individual needs to allow the stories within to flow up and out, so do the cultures we live among. Groups of people should have their own myths and tales for how death is interacting with them and living among them. Without the myths, we stand in a repressed silence that is not there because it is superior to or beyond myth making capacity. It is silent because it fears to risk. This fear represses the possible myths and as we stated before, repressed myths or things that we do not allow to come up and out of us, kill us. Have you looked into your own culturally relevant myths?

We have somehow learned the belief that silently staring off into the sunset, without a word to say means we have risen above the need for something. First, it may mean that we may not have any idea what to say or where to begin to dig for what it is we should say. Second, it may mean that we are not willing to risk saying something in front of others. Both of these are nothing but silence filled with fear. That is not a deep silence built on wisdom. The silence we need to learn in this day and age of multiculturalism is a silence that exists because it is listening deeply to what "others" have to offer. It is a silence that is in wonder and awe of what comes out of people and it is a silence that is allowing that "stuff" of the other to impact them in a way that is engaging and not reactionary.

People will always disbelieve and be at odds with other peoples' beliefs and myths. It is natural because one person is not the other person—they are (culturally and socially) individual selves. This acknowledgement of being individual is an acknowledgement of the "not-the-same-ness" which underlies divergent beliefs.

There will be things that people value that will just plain be different from what you value and some of those values may be a threat to your being. Those things will be the hardest to tolerate and try to come to terms with. But, this is no reason for people to constantly posture themselves as reactionary. It is far better to engage individual and cultural diversity with inquiry and openness so we can see to the root of the issues and identify the similarities that underlie our human experience. All in all, sometimes we will be able to live up to this pinnacle of human acceptance and at other times we will fail miserably.

Humanity and cultures move ahead slowly in the process of culling out what is unhealthy and unnecessary. It takes aeons for us to synthesize and align toward health, and in the process we will

Chapter Five

make countless errors. But, I do believe in the long haul we are able to exist and even flourish in and among a multiplicity of belief and emotion. It is simply a lot of hard work.

In a nation that has been working with the melting pot experiment a lot longer than most; we are still learning our way around divergent beliefs. This whole issue of an ability to tolerate and even respect divergent beliefs has been critical in the hospice movement.

In hospice, because it is not a denominational or partisan based organization (for the most part) that touts a systematic theology of its own, it has created a space within which individual belief and emotion can not only be tolerated, but fostered and nourished. The spiritual care workers in hospice listen deeply to the stories that come up and out of the patients and families; they listen with a wonder and respect that is more than just a gritting-of-the-teeth-allowance. They actually listen with an openness that is nurturing. Their concerned inquiry actually waters the divergent growth in others.

This is how I know it is possible for others. I have seen it with my own eyes. I have felt it with my own soul. I have heard it with my own ears. Mutual growth and development can occur amid divergent belief and feeling. In fact, once you start to allow the free exchange of emotions and beliefs, you will find that the idiosyncrasies that you immediately identify as divergent in your own understanding of the way life works are really only the fluff of the story. Eventually those things fall away and you come up against some core fears, hopes, and longings that express the great underground river of human existence that unites us all. You find that there are underpinnings that are identical.

Joe was in his early sixties. He had just retired and moved to a house he and his wife had had built for this new passage in their lives: retirement. They moved in and he found out he had advanced lung disease and had six month to live—at best. Their foundation crumbled.

Lung disease tends to metastasize to the brain, so I knew we had a minimal amount of time to work with the family before Joe was unable to participate in things in the way the family had come to expect that he could and would. He would become someone different before he died.

This change in people as they approach death can be very unnerving, unsettling, and disturbing for loved ones to witness. It often is so strong a presence in the dying process that it throws people off track from doing and saying things that they really want to do and say. It forces people to take mutant side trips in life's journey—bumping them off the main trail that they thought they were on. This complicates the grieving process and often causes regrets once death has occurred.

Another thing that subverts the process at the end of life is the daunting and looming presence of insurance companies and healthcare providers telling you what you can and cannot do. Many of the instructions and demands are counter to the ways people have lived their whole lives and become impediments and barriers to dying well. The hospice movement has remediated these disparities by intervening in family situations to help them get back on track with living the way they have and dying well without this roadblocks.

I began identifying for Joe and his family that things could change in his ability to communicate and function in and among the family in ways he had in the past; particularly as the disease progressed. I shared this with them verbally. I told them he may begin to forget things or remember things differently than others. He may see things that other people do not see (these visual disturbances in the dying range from seeing things float in front of them like words or butterflies all the way to seeing people they knew or loved—especially those who have already died).

Chapter Five

He may also begin to talk about things as if he was in a deep sleep or dream state—they would be imagistic statements sounding like he was experiencing some other reality. All of this is very common in the dying and in particular when disease progression intensifies (I am not willing to say that it is only in brain metastases). They tolerated this discussion well. The whole family had run out and read Elisabeth Kubler-Ross's *On Death and Dying* as soon as they got the prognosis. They were open to the process.

I made sure that the nurse had spoken to the family about signs and symptoms of approaching death and signs and symptoms of his specific disease progression. She had, so the family had sufficient knowledge at their fingertips about what was going on and what could come to pass.

As is generally the case in the beginning of spiritual care in hospice, I asked them a series of open ended questions. What have the doctors told you? Do you understand what is going on? Are you afraid? What are your concerns? Folks can jump into these questions on many different levels. They can answer them about physical issues or go right into psycho-social-spiritual issues. They can answer about what they are immediately afraid of, or they can delve into existential dread.

In this case Joe jumped into the most pragmatic. He said he was afraid that his grandchildren would come in some morning and find him dead. He had moved into his daughters home after the news was shared. He knew that one possible outcome was that he would bleed out and he did not want the kids to see this.

I had to ask a few more probing questions to get him to state his concern this clearly, but when he did, we were able to take a look at equally pragmatic responses to this type of fear. We could use dark colored sheets to hide the dramatic visual image that blood on white sheets would provoke. We could make sure that the grandchildren came to their grandmother first and asked if it was ok to see grandpa.

DANSE MACABRE

Both of these things settled Joe and the whole family. The silent tension in the family shifted and they began to ask questions. This shift happened because they were able to elicit the fear that they had all held and verbalize it. Once this is done, people are ready to move toward a solution.

It takes care not to rush the process and also not to verbalize the answer yourself. The people at the center of the process need to carve and own the words about the fear and then they can hear solutions. It takes prompting and direction and a deep listening, but that is how the process is able to move ahead.

As the days wore on I was called back to the home. Joe had started to say things that did not make sense to the family and then he stopped talking altogether. I figured that he had become embarrassed by the things he was saying and that he just simply decided not to talk. But, I had to get him to be able to identify this and share it with the family if their process was to be validated. After an hour of sitting with Joe and making small talk, he said something that did not fit into the conversation and then he reached up to grab something that he saw pass by in front of him. As soon as he did this, I asked, "Is that why you have stopped talking to your family? Because you see and say things like that?" He responded immediately, "Yup!"

I acknowledged that this had to be tough, especially since his greatest fear is how the family would "find him". This was really a continuation of that same issue for him. He did not want to be found crazy by his grandchildren, or to be found a bloody mess. We needed to pursuit the issue a bit further as the air surrounding the issue did not seem to be settled or clear. He still was very disturbed by something, but it was not clear what it was.

When the issues get like this, I fall back on simple and open ended questions. It helps give people some room within which to verbally wander until everyone can start to get a bearing on what it is that is coming up and out. At some point he mentioned death and I asked him what death looked like to him. He responded immediately with an answer that almost seemed to come up and out of him without his permission or cognitive assent. He said, "It is coming at me from the left and carrying a bag."

That is a classic telling. That is something coming up and out of an individual that is critical for saving them. That is what is sounds like. The unconscious burps up these things that sound mythological and poetic, like they are part of a dreamscape. These little nuggets have everything to do with our healing in life. I knew that.

I asked Joe to believe me when I told him that what he just said was not crazy but that it was something very important for him to be able to figure out if he was to die well. That what he had said may have been aided by the loosening up of the ego that occurs with dying and also disease progression, but that it was not craziness. It was something he was trying to communicate to himself. He agreed and let me share this valuable info with the family. We sat around for a while trying to interpret this message, but did not come up with anything that felt like it was valid.

I told them all that I trusted we would find out what this meant and I asked them to trust as well. They agreed and I believe it was their faith and trust that produced the interpretation we were all looking for. Their participation in this process made a difference.

Five days later I got a call. "Father Tom, we found it." "Found what," I countered. "We found the bag," they said. "In the closet in Dad's room—on the LEFT hand side of the room—we found a brown paper bag. When we took it out to see what was in it, Dad said, "That's the BAG." We opened it to find an urn inside of it; an urn that housed his mother's remains." "I was supposed to scatter those," he told us. "I can't believe I forgot."

Now we had something that was of personal importance to the patient and the family. They distributed Joe's mother's ashes. He was able to relax. They all had a time of sharing family memories, forgiveness, and hope and then a few days later Joe died peacefully; alone in his room. The grandchildren did not find him, his wife did.

DANSE MACABRE

This is a small but poignant example of the kinds of things housed in the sub and unconscious. These are the things that need to come up and out in order to save us; things that make up our personal mythologies. These are movement and growth at death.

Chapter Six

Our modern digital and technological world has a set of assumptions and beliefs that come along with it. These assumptions and beliefs have taken up residence in us and begun to establish an unspoken mythology. We rarely verbalize this mythology and because of that it often rears up and subverts other deeper and more personal beliefs and feelings.

The mythology of medical technology is strong; the mythology of humanity is weak. We believe that our medicine and tools can keep us alive forever. We believe that there will always be a cure. We believe that looking for a remedy is more important than enjoying what we have right now. We can just hold on to life a bit more if we run this one final experiment. Our hope lies in liquids and needles and gadgets.

This is something we have fallen into believing gradually over time. Slowly we have seen how this one time and that one time medicine and technology has worked, so we build an unspoken agreement and belief that we can always depend on medicine and technology to sustain us. It is a way of diverting our attention from the reality of dying. It is also a denial that can cost us valuable time.

Many people spend more and more time trying to cure their dying instead of doing things they feel they need to before they die. Instead of talking with their children, they are running to doctors offices. Instead of asking for forgiveness they have one more test to get to—one they must undergo by themselves.

I am not saying these things may or can not help. I am saying we tend to be managed by our technology and medicine. We do not tend to manage them. Who will stand up and give families permission to say, "No more! We need to spend time together before you die."

It is not just the amount of time that our medicine and technology consume. Quite often we are not ourselves—we become different people—after all of the surgeries, drugs, procedures, and therapies. Our lives and even our daily living is somehow altered by the prolonging of our lives. Some of that comes from shear fatigue.

You become so physically and emotionally drained from all of the constant invasion. Some of the invasion is physical—foreign things being poked and prodded into your body. Some of the invasion is psycho-social—people constantly in your face and in your life thinking they have or should have access to each and every one of the deep recesses of your existence. It just is not healthy. You are worn down; and, in being worn down you are susceptible to becoming "other" than who you would like or choose to be.

We are beginning to realize that we just can't do everything possible and call that living. For one thing, people just can't pay for every option—even with insurance. Managed care is helping us sort that out. They are only willing to pay for so much.

Beyond that, though, we are coming to the end of our ability to believe in salvation by gadgets. We have seen enough to know something is a bit off kilter. We are beginning to feel that bells and whistles may be a red herring after all. It may be the economics of the medical industry has pushed us into waking up, but I would like to think that some people just began to realize we are "more than our bodies". We have a quality to our lives that is impeded by the constant and ongoing diversion that "heroic measures" add to our days.

Chapter Six

Who have I Become; A Sudden Change of Heart

Today
I am a new
man, a new heart beats
in my chest.
Yesterday
it—the heart—
was his, but now it is
mine. Now it takes
my blood in and
sends it out to all the
places I have allowed
it to go with my old
heart. But,
today
is different. I went to
eat some asparagus and
the smell of it made
me sick. I used to love
asparagus. I am thirsty for
coffee and I have never
liked the stuff until now.

I don't trust the nurse and
I just don't know why.

It seems there are changes
happening in me; changes I
do not understand. I don't know
that the man I am becoming now
will get along with the man
I used to be.

DANSE MACABRE

And what has become
of him? The man who's
heart I now hold. Do they
sew my heart into
his lifeless body, so he
does not get to the River
Styx without a muscle
beating in his dead chest?

Why now, why at this
pass in my life?

This change of heart is really
a change of heart; and,

I am not
sure who gets to stay.

There is a space around and within the dying that is both liminal and luminal. It is liminal because it is a threshold of change and transformation; a battle ground for life altering passages. It is luminal because everything becomes clear in the light of the experience of approaching death; everything is seen for what it is.

It takes a while to get used to this environment that surrounds approaching death. It so pervades the dying that they often appear to be new creatures to those who have known them their whole life. There is something different about them. It is the reason abrupt silence pervades the deathbed. People sense a clarity and a shifting of meaning. Of course, this makes many people afraid. But, something is going on in the space surrounding those who are getting ready to leave the planet.

The space surrounding the dying is also filled with a lot of activity. There is a lot of work that goes on at the end-of-life when we have a fair warning that we are going die. People spend a lot

Chapter Six

of time and energy putting their house in order, repairing relationships, exploring spiritual issues they had laid aside for later, reconnecting with God and of course asking for forgiveness. It was one of the things I loved about hospice work: people were serious about working on themselves. You always had better results in therapeutic and formation work.

I will never forget Raymond. He was the first hospice patient I visited. He was dying from end-stage HIV. He was so thin and so frail; but his room was filled with an immense sense of presence that I could not figure out. Later I came to know this presence as the light; it is the light of the dying.

This light of the dying is not necessarily visible. It has some qualities that simply make it astounding and understandable at the same time. When the Tibetan's speak about the "clear light", I imagine that this is what they mean. Everything in this space is "clear". Death brings clarity and clarification. But, you must be attentive to it.

Let me rework that last statement. It is not that you are not attentive to the clear light surrounding death (and life for that matter), because I think everyone is attentive or aware of it. That is why some people run from the deathbed. The presence of the stillness and silence of the clear light is like a deafening white-noise to some. They either try to escape it or lean all sorts of diversions up against it in the hopes that they can hide it.

What it is that is lacking is a surrender to the awareness of the clear light; an acceptance of the ever-present "now-ness" of things. People tend to squirm in the vicinity of this clarity. People are uncomfortable with the great silence. They like to keep busy. But, what can eventually come to pass is that we can learn to give the ineffable nod of the affirmative in the presence of the clear light. We can live in the unbridled acknowledgement of the Here and Now, not just flee its presence and hide from its view.

I think that gives better witness to what I was hoping to say.

DANSE MACABRE

I had a lot of immediate adverse reactions around Raymond. First, I had to suit up with mask, gloves and gown when I went to see him. I was not prepared for that. I felt so odd. I thought I was taking preparations that you needed to take when going to another planet or into a radioactive environment. Going in a room to pray and sing with a man who was dying, frail, and unconscious really did not seem to warrant this kind of protection. But I had to if I was to visit.

Then there was the loneliness. Perhaps because you had to suit up to see him; perhaps because he had AIDS; regardless, no one came near his room let alone into his room to visit with him. It was as if we had been set adrift from all mankind. That is how Raymond died; peaceful and alone.

While I was with him that day he reached out several times to grab things. Even though he was unconscious, he reached out. This is called terminal agitation. Even when he became conscious (on later visits) he continued to reach out for things; grabbing to hold them with his fingers and thumb. I had asked him what he was grabbing. He told me, "Butterflies".

It was at that point that I decided I liked the responses the dying gave to questions about their experiences—as opposed to the explanations that the professionals gave. The dying had simple answers. Their answers made sense. Butterflies always make sense over terminal agitation.

There were some other things that emerged that I did not like. I did not like how people stood around talking about patients as if they were unable to hear. At the nurse's stations the sound of "blah-blah-blah-personal-opinions" arose from the shuffling of notes and patient charts. You could get caught up on just about any patient's life and case history if you cared to.

Chapter Six

This was before the privacy practice diversion. All those papers that people have to sign and all of the policies that were to have been put in place never once stopped a secretary or healthcare professional from sharing their opinion about a person or a case at a decibel that was clearly beyond the range of anyone's' definition of "privacy". It still goes on.

I did not and still do not like how people swoop in on the dying and carry away their belongings long before they are dead. I saw it often.

There is a clip from the movie "Zorba the Greek" that shows people carrying off the belongings of a woman who is "not-dead-yet". They enter her home and cart off stuff while she is dying in her bed upstairs. It happens all of the time. They are not just carting off "stuff". They are dragging away dignity and worth as well.

I had brought a small tape player to Raymond so he could have music playing. I asked the staff to turn it on occasionally for him. The next day I came back and it was gone. No one had any idea what had happened to it.

These simple issues need to be rectified in care settings. These little things make the environments inhumane. People should not feel set upon as carrion when they are in care settings.

This dividing up of the spoils of the dying is a classic example of people squirming in the presence of the clear light. Rather than hallow the sense of depth that is exposed in the clear light, people attempt to dismantle and cart it off. And they call us "thinking man". Yeah, right.

The other pieces of the issues that surround the dying in care settings are that they start to lose their voice early on in the process and they also lose their independence. One of the most disheartening things to watch happen is watching a person lose their ability to stay in their own home because they are unable to care for themselves. But then, add insult to injury, they may then get moved half way across the state (far from any loved one who would want to spend time with them) because of issues surrounding payment.

DANSE MACABRE

"The only place we have a "such-and-such bed" available for the patient is in "East Jabip". I have heard it and seen it too many times. Not only is the place out of reach for friends and relatives, it is a whole new environment for the dying person. Who wants to die in some new town, in some new home, in a bed that is not yours? Not me.

Pulling Down the Light

It is the way the autumn
leaves pull the light down
 to the ground
that I have been noticing lately.

It comes to be the same with
 all dyings,
with all deaths.

It is the way they reflect their brightness
 to the corners of my eyes
and their dappled colors to my heart.

That is the way their dying goes.
Pulling down
 great bunches of the light
 right before
 they fall
 to the ground
 and die and become the earth
 upon which we all stand.

Chapter Six

Raymond's Death

I can still feel the
surprise
of smelling my 7th grade
guidance counselor
last week;

and my 5th grade history
teacher
the month before.

I can feel it because
two days ago,
the smell of
fresh plantain in
the warm mist of rain
took me by the arm
to my boyhood fishing;

and today I smelled
Raymond's hair-grease
on the way back from
watching him die and
holding his hand. Watching
him die alone, there,
by himself,
with no family
or friends. I stayed
longer than usual;
watching him reach and point
and stare off into space,
calling for help.

DANSE MACABRE

Too many die alone,
I cannot stay for them all,
but I did for him;

I did today.

Raymond died a few weeks after I started visits with him. He died in a nursing care facility that was about one hundred miles away from his home and family. He died in a room by himself because when the other Medicaid patient in his room found out he had AIDS, he wanted to be moved. Raymond was left to be alone. Raymond was left alone.

I tried to get there every day those last few days, so he had some decreased isolation. I sang him hymns—hymns his family told me he loved. He died on the weekend while I was home with my wife and children. No one called me. He was buried quickly with no fanfare.

It rattled me because it just seemed so unfair. I had no idea that most of life would turn out to be this way. Most of everyone's lives would turn out to be this way. The mythic dream that we had called the "American Dream" growing up had started to unravel somewhere in the mid seventies. Somewhere in the late nineties people along the edge of our culture where starting to fall through the cracks again. Raymond was clearly one of those people. He was too gentle a soul to have been treated that way.

Chapter Seven

A LOT of days I felt Death breathing down my neck, like that first day when I felt him near while I was putting on my socks. I could look over my shoulder as I tied my shoe. I could look into the place I felt His looming pall. That awareness passed into a silent recognition, and that recognition was my nod, my hello to Him that day. He knew I knew He was there. That was a good place to begin.

He was not there for me. That is, He was not there to lure me into His clutches that day or any day. He was not there because it was my turn to die. He was there because He followed me most days: He or His countless minions.

Often, actually, most often, Death would catch up with me somewhere on the road. I would feel His presence somewhere on my way to work. But, that one day (the day I noticed Him while putting on my socks), it was different. He actually met me at home; my home. I did not know that I liked Him being there. When I did, I did not say so.

I finished getting ready, that day and then left. He stayed with me. He usually stayed with me until the last traces of my work had left my thoughts, left my feelings, and left my hopes. He usually stayed with me until I was done writing my last note for the last patient of the day; after scrubbing Him off my hands with alcohol.

He followed me because I cared for His children. I cared for the dying. Even though they were not His children yet—not until their breath ceased its cycle—they would join Him. They would join Him when they ended up where they came from: the ground.

DANSE MACABRE

Another reminder that T. S. Eliot was right: "our ending is our beginning."

The ground is not such a horrible destiny. It is where my people are. It is where everything is. I squeeze a handful of soil in my fist and can feel my angelic side, my humanity, and my connection with all that is, my connection with all that is to come, and my connection with all that has already come undone.

I am the ground. And, as if my intuition is not enough, science has shown that everything is in the dirt. What has been discovered in the humus under foot is nothing less than everything—again proving Eliot and his "fear in a handful of dust." Someone should reconsider Eliot. He knew something; Blake, too.

One day I saw Death dancing.

There were other times I had seen Him since that first day at my side while tying shoes. But, this one day was the first dance I saw Him do. He swirled around this one guy—animating his conversation. He went in and through this man—apparently working him like a marionette.

He was dancing all around Henry. Slowly, at first he danced. Then the slow dancing seemed to deepen, taking on the quality of gliding—a sort of stalking about his prey; slowly, slowly circling, building speed. Somewhere in the swirling He popped right into Henry and danced him. Henry's arms began to lilt gracefully like he was moving to some cosmic cello music. Then, he went limp again.

I can usually ignore Him at first. It is my urge to take away his sense of self-importance. By the time He is whirling and spinning at a quick and steady clip, I am not only ready to acknowledge Him, but am unable to keep my eyes off of Him.

I am mesmerized by the beauty and rhythm of His movement. It is entrancing. And when He enters His prey and dances them; well, forget about it. You just cannot take your eyes off of Him.

Chapter Seven

When He was done, Henry sat there, still, on the couch.

Henry—or at this point what simply seemed like Henry's body alone—reclined back over its length, gulping at the air and haggling with himself—more than with me—about meaning and worth and value. He was muttering things to himself.

It was in that reclined draping that Death entered him and danced him. There was fluidity to his stillness and gulping that let me know he was being danced. His arms started moving gracefully again.

He reeled out the story of his life. He was seemingly telling me, but more of it was his telling himself. Moving within his own life, he did not notice my entrancement with Death's dancing in and out, over and around and under his words, and tales, and stories and gasps. Henry was sometimes alert and sometimes just muttering his tale. That is clearly what made it seem Death was entering and exiting him, dancing him again and again.

It was a synchronized display of past and present and future. It was a display that was giving flesh to the invisibility of his words and groans. All of it was unbeknownst to the very person at the center of the dance itself. Unbeknownst to the one whose dance I watched; unbeknownst to the man fighting to breathe. He told the story of his life; he muttered the question of his life.

For two and a half hours he gasped and pondered and asked me again and again and again, "What could I do?" He did not want an answer. It was clear that his speaking to me was not for me. It was for himself. He was telling me for himself.

Henry felt he had had no real choices in life. He had chosen what he was supposed to have chosen. And that was that. His arms would gracefully dance in the air. He would emphatically gesture to me about something he knew made sense to him. I had no idea what he was talking about. And then, he would ask me, "What could I do"?

The whole scene was sort of like a theatre of the absurd performance. I expected Eugene Ionesco to walk into the room and describe the scene I had just watched; or, at least Woody Allen. Instead, all I got was to help walk a naked man back to bed, while supporting his skeletal frame and moving slower than I had ever cared to move.

Death danced His macabre dance all around Henry—all within Henry. The curtains were drawn, no lights were on, and He danced. Henry lay there gasping, no clothes on. He lay there with his boxers draped over his genitals. He was too weak to dress. I have no idea how he had gotten himself to the couch, but it was clear that he could not get up and back into bed without my assistance.

He was dying and Death was dancing.

Death danced and danced and danced. Henry mused.

You got the sense they had been doing this forever, they were so comfortable in each other's presence.

Eventually, he knew Death was there. He could feel the breeze of his whirling, or he sensed His closeness because he would pause and look in the direction of the movement. He would cock his head to the side, as if he noticed something askew, something different, a shift in reality. But, then he would return to his banter, musing and musing, and Death kept dancing.

OK, so there are two times I knew that Death was close. One time was when I was getting dressed. And another time was with a naked man on the sofa. Not a great book premise. But, that's the point. Why don't books talk about us seeing Death?

I think it is because we have killed our myth making ability and our very concern to see ourselves about the process of making myths. We really do not care. That, and the fact that we don't want to be considered mad by other people. I have lost that fear: years ago.

Why do we not sit around and tell tales any more? What has shifted inside us? Have we crossed over some threshold in our own

Chapter Seven

development? Have we become so driven to consume that we do not feel the need to sit around the fire and tell tales? Have we no use for the useless?

It usually takes a few hours to recover from these sessions with patients. The immense intensity of the experiences really takes the energy out of you. I tend to be in an altered state when I get done. It is like being flown through a time warp two or three times in an hour. It takes It out of you.

I try to get some caffeine or food into my system. This brings me back to the immediate and local form of existence. Food and coffee ground me. Being non-local too long can prove troublesome. You can write and meditate well; you can also be an open resource for healing and therapeutic mending, but you can't play cards, talk politics, drive a vehicle, or do small talk.

It is not just Death's dance and Henry's unburdening of soul that makes a body go non-local. It is the sum of both; and, all the rest. It is the whole visit of the living and the dead that comes to bear on the local and smear it into non-locality.

I am really glad that not everyone is given to share these appalling apparitions. It would kill the planet, or at least expand the boundaries of the universe too rapidly, driving it over the edge of itself. These are powerful. Tender moments at times, sad at times, but always powerful. It would; however, be good to hear people mentioning these things every once in a while, though.

In Death's dancing comes the unwinding of the days of a man's life. People learn to weave the tapestry of their life into their pores and cells. As the end approaches they review the pores and cells and tell the tales written there; Death dances to the music of the story.

Choreographed from the dawn of time, each man's tale is different and yet enough the same that there is never a pause in Death's step. He misses no beat because of surprise or horror; as if He has heard it all. He dances on.

DANSE MACABRE

This is powerfully draining. And, most people do not even know this is going on. They just feel something odd when they are with the dying. They have no idea it is so personal. They have no idea it will happen to them. Or, so they pretend. Remember, I believe we are all aware of these things. We just do not surrender to their reality.

I knew about the dance clearly from my third grade year on. I had an inkling of it in first grade, though. I was exposed to the idea of the myth about Death doing His dance around Halloween each year.

The Dance of Death

"Tap, tap, and tap,
Death sits on the tombstone and drums with his heel.
Tap, tap, and tap,
Death tunes up his fiddle and plays a weird reel
Tap, tap and tap on his violin.
'Tis midnight and sadly the winter wind moans;
From shadowy lindens, with loud sighs and groans,
The skeleton dancers in white, whirling crowds
Come leaping and skipping and waving their shrouds.
Tap, tap, and tap, what a horrible sound –
The rattle of the bones as they dance 'round and 'round!
But hark! Behold young chanticleer heralds the day
And Death and his dancers have vanished away.
Tap, tap, and tap."
—Henri Cazalis, 1840–1909

". . . Tap, tap and tap."
There was an odd circuitousness about that poem. I had come to live the lines of the poem in my hospice work with the dying.

Chapter Seven

That was half of the circle. I got to see the words of Cazalis in real life. Death animated the people and the space around the work I did and the Dance of Death was the stuff of my existence. But it began earlier in my life. The first half of the circle began in the first half of my life—in my childhood

This other half of the circle—the childhood portion of my life—was haunted by the poem by Henri Cazalis. This poem had entered my life as a child and had been rattling around inside of me—for whatever reason—until now. I loved that poem and the music that Charles-Camille Saint-Saëns had set the poem to in 1874 when he wrote his tone poem. I found it important, chilling, and captivating—all at once.

When I was young I was given the opportunity to listen to the music and words of the tone poem every year. Our class would listen to the teacher read the poem, play the music, and then show us a filmstrip that combined the music with some water colors of a contemporary artist. It still haunts my heart as my interior mind replays the images of the elementary school's filmstrip. It makes me wonder if I had loved it so much because I would do hospice work later on in life; or did I go on to do hospice work because I loved it so much.

Each autumn as Halloween drew near, the school music teacher—who used to roam from room to room with her AV cart—would wander into our class with the "Dance of Death". This had been going on since first grade in 1968. I remember it most vividly in third grade.

My third grade teacher had been a keen friend of my grandmother's. Mom-mom had been dead for years and this teacher had watched out for me at school—a duty performed for her dead friend. It was when this came together for me—the teacher that represented my grandmother (and her death) and the filmstrip on the dance of death—that I was able to start and process Mom-mom's death.

DANSE MACABRE

It took both of them in close proximity for me to begin to develop a sense to death. I believe it was because the art form of the music, poem, and paintings gave me a concrete myth to connect death to. It gave me an archetype of death—which until then had only been a word concept and a missing grandmother. A young boy cannot understand this liminal and luminal space without a myth. Without a myth liminal and luminal space is strictly conceptual.

My connection with this teacher was already wrapped up and in a relationship caused by death. When the bone dance showed up on the curriculum the year she was my teacher it was old home week. I knew she loved my grandmother. Every time I saw her, I could feel my dead grandmother's presence.

And so, Death got hardwired into my life when the death of my grandmother got married to this filmstrip. I got to see the myth of Death before my very eyes. Now I could figure out what happened to Mom-mom.

". . . Tap, tap and tap."

When the school gave me the gift of Dance Macabre, they gave me a gift that would impress me for life. The filmstrip would show up in our yearly curriculum for some time. It was a familiar event every year until 6th grade, or maybe 7th. Every year I saw it I espoused the myth anew.

There was nothing horrific about it. It was just a Halloween song and filmstrip. There was one for Thanksgiving, and Christmas, Easter and the Patriotic Holidays. We did songs and filmstrips to check off the little box on our report card that showed "Music". It was not maudlin.

What took away our desire to see children process these things? Why did we stop fabricating myths and yarns, and tales? What has happened to us?

Today, I am sure there would need to be a liability waiver or correctness disclaimer or some "don't-want-to-offend-you-note". That is just what we do, today. That is who we have become.

Chapter Seven

"... Tap, tap and tap."

"Gawd", what a shallow lot we are. We bitch and bicker about so much minutiae that we never notice someone walking off with our myths. But they did. Clearly, somewhere between my seventh grade and the year 1995 or maybe 1994 that is what happened. Someone or "some-group-of-someone-s" walked right off with all our myths.

They had been alive in third grade. I know that because that was the year men walked on the moon and said amazing things about small steps and giant steps. That was myth. I remember that clearly. But, it started to die in the mid seventies and it was "most sincerely dead" by the mid nineties. Who stole our mythmaking?

It probably was being undermined or a plot was being made back when people felt how horrible America had become. Back when some people thought it was OK to kill John Kennedy, Bobby Kennedy, Martin Luther King and Malcolm X.

Some big and important people planned those deaths; some people who were supposed to know better. People we may have been trusting.

You start to lose your ability to believe in myths when they start killing the giants. When people began to tear at Camelot that is when we began losing our hope. And, what synched the disbelief was the notion that perhaps the powers that be were behind these atrocities.

Why would you want to believe myths when the real guys, the real agencies that sneak about and play leadership may have been involved in taking away the giants?

By the sixth or seventh grade they stopped the filmstrip. Clearly, something had shifted or was in the process of shifting. Things became radically different for mankind—at least the American version of mankind. Our myths and our mythmaking seems to have stopped.

Viet Nam may have been one of the last straws. Watergate started crushing our spirits. Then technology took over. All of these events have the telltale signs of material that could be woven into myth. But they were never really integrated into our cultural psyche with any sense of resolution. Something was clearly already dead in our modern life—or at least well on its way to being clearly dead.

We couldn't trust leaders anymore, so maybe technology would be the pill. We built whole new orders of structure and they became the rave. We started a mythology that would go underground. We were colluding with robots and machines because clearly our society and its leaders could not be trusted. Technology appeared to lack the moral confusion, greed, and oppression that we grew to live in fear of.

Even though we birth awesome science fiction from the halls of technological development, we have not gone back to myths for our sustenance. Star Wars, Dune and the rest of them are all good stories, but we lost our ability to trust the story-tellers when JFK was shot. The stories were epic, but we had no trustable culture to hang them on. The infrastructure turned out to be corrupt.

When your storytellers can't be trusted, then you know myth is dead.

Now, the stories live with marginal import and power. But, we cast them aside when a new one is told, never seeking to bring them together and weave out integrated meanings. That is what myth-making is for. It gives us an oral/aural flannelgraph board on which to arrange and rearrange our current understanding of how everything fits together. It explains how one thing is over and against how another thing is.

That is gone for us—perhaps forever. Somehow we used to do better at holding the myths together. Maybe neighborhoods and societies have changed forever. I still think people need those myths.

"... Tap, tap and tap."

Chapter Eight

Before I had begun this rhythmic and steady walk with Death I had had inklings of its unraveling nature and capability. I had unknowingly rambled amid Death's ability to dissolve things in the years leading up to my thirty-fourth birthday.

At the age of thirty-four I watched my father disintegrate. He began his falling apart. His body—which had had any number of catastrophes happen on and in it—was no longer able to mend and work towards growth the way it had before.

As a matter of fact, neither could his mind. His body and person were no longer able to put themselves back together again. Humpty-Dumpty lost. I really had thought there might be a Humpty-Dumpty regained in our future. I was mistaken. He had begun the process of stopping.

He did not come to full stop all at once, but began to slowly undo. He began to disintegrate; to UN-integrate. Entropy was having its way.

Not only is the universe falling apart, coming unglued, dropping away, unwinding and undoing itself, but my father was as well. And, if I had thought about it then, I was too.

It was like he had been heading in one direction and then he began to slow down and do a turnabout—heading in the opposite direction; back to the earth. He was walking away from being a separate being from the earth. He was getting ready to become earth again.

Hold the dirt. You are in there. And so are all your ancestors. Feel them. Feel everything in the dirt that has been tall and mighty and alive, but has come undone. Feel everything that lost its form and fell back down to the ground—upon which we stand.

I think we get to see a lot more of this unwinding today. In the days gone by people tended to have large events that caused them to die all at once. Now, we have the technology to bring people back to life.

With the heavy use of synthetics and pharmacopeias we are able to patch people together and extend their existence further into the future. People can move ahead and peter-out again and again and again until we say, "Enough."

I am not sure about the Promethean skill we have garnered from all of our research and newly honed abilities. I am not sure I believe it is good to prolong peoples' lives over and over again.

This techno-crazed medicinal phenomenon is what saved my father—one calamity after another. Without this blessed skill he would have died straightway and been done with it. Instead, he slowly diminished over time; becoming less of who he had been (and who he had wished to be) with each passing incident. He became less able to cope with his decline.

By the time I had noticed that he had been falling apart, I had become sick of the process. It had been eating at me and at him for years. Dying, and dying again over too long of a period seems to wear down everything in its wake. Without being able to sort out the myth of what is happening, without a space where it is sacred to tell the tales, people live with this perpetual erosion of character and fortitude until they are ghosts living in the flatland.

Enter T.S. Eliot. Eliot sensed this movement toward a grey landscape that robotically assigned neutral value and meaning to everything.

Chapter Eight

By the time he actually died, I was tired of him dying. In truth, he died again and again and again. Give me a single event, please.

His prostate had become the center of his world. For some time before that, his knee was the center. Before that it was a stroke that had taken him to the ground, and the angioplasty, and an aneurysm, a burst femur; and, one trip after another he left. Each time a new center.

There had also been numerous hospitalizations for depression, attempted suicides, and also a heart attack. Multiple attempts at suicide should have been seen as his attempt to stop the madness.

What must someone do to earn this sort of visit from the angel of Death, or at least the angel of severe bodily rejection and harm? Maybe this is the way it will be for the new man of the 21st century—a jiffy lube of medical repairs.

It scares me. A horror settles into my bones that is greater than the thought of non-existence. Who pays Death to linger so long? What insurance policy pays for Him to go away and come back, go away and come back? If some insurance executive catches onto these billable moments, you can bet we'll see a reduction of sinkable episodes.

Each one of these onslaughts seems to have opened a door for a part of him to leave or escape through. Sometimes something physical left him—clear speech, or a strong gate; other times it was emotional.

Where it goes I do not know. But it leaves—this much I am sure of. Pieces of him began leaving. Soon I had no idea who he was anymore.

Most of us wish we had some way to grab hold of this process of calamity that happens to us. We wish we could make it stop. We cannot. It is this silent fear that lives under the surface of everyday life. It tends to keeps us just a bit too subdued a bit, too rational.

DANSE MACABRE

I think we feel we can outsmart the disasters with logical and steady living. It is not so. Death and diminishment are not proud. They will come to us all; when they wish.

Because we cannot control this calamity, this helplessness, we hide from it. It is a horrible thing to acknowledge. It is—so we believe—better not to look at it. Surely then it will leave us. It is not so.

It took me several years to find out what was genuinely revolting me about Dad's diminishings. It had some connection to his complaining I am sure.

It also had something to do with his self-absorption. I believe the pulsing, and throbbing core of it had to do with his helplessness. It is an ever-present reminder that this is how it is—for us all. We are really all just danced by someone else—gasping like Henry strewn on the couch of our dying.

My father could not keep his center. I blamed him for that. Each event drew him further away from his own self. He was changing without the desire, will, or attempt to change. I blamed him that he did not fight hard enough to keep the changes at bay—or fight at all.

I know now that that loss of will or passion is a part of what we become when technology saves us again and again. It is as if each time technology brings us back to human life, a piece of us turns into technology. Slowly morphed over dozens of procedures, we become the technology we build.

I had a hard time sitting still and watching him be helpless and watching me become helpless about my feelings of helplessness for him. The depth of my revulsion was an astounding tribute to the complexities of the mind and the heart.

Not only are we able to think and feel helpless, but we are also capable of reflecting back on that thought and feeling and think and feel helpless about that state itself.

Chapter Eight

This is what sets us above the other animals—we are self-reflexive. We are able to beat ourselves into the ground with our own ability to think and or beat.

And so, in 1995, my thirty-fourth year, I felt helpless about my father's helplessness with his coming apart—slowly coming apart. This is a major thing to wake up and discover that is going on for you, in your life—just below the surface. It is the kind of stuff that we love to shove deeper down and deeper in. But, as we know, that kills us.

This seems to be around the same time that I noticed that social myths were clearly dead. Society had shifted and we were no longer telling tales to get along. Perhaps it was just my father that died for me that year. I mean, he lived until 2000, but he was definitely dead to me as I had known him in 1995. I think the unwinding of my father helped me to notice that the infrastructure of our society had also come undone.

I was feeling helpless about Death approaching. That feeling is a large part of what is back behind our notion of Death. Everything is built on a big fear that is best left unsaid; best left unspoken. As we all know; if we don't speak it, it is not real. We are genuinely helpless in the face of Death.

What do you do with all of that? How do you handle it? How long can you sit with that kind of intensity before you just snap? If you don't snap you may just get a major addiction out of it, or have 3-5 kids all in a row or just numb out by working all of the time.

I am not so sure that we are wired to handle this type of death and dying in the techno-age. These days' people don't just die; they tend to linger.

People now peter out. The energizer bunny has become an icon for this generation's meaning behind life. It is not very deep or very noble; what matters is that we don't stop, but keep on going.

That is consuming. It means a person can die a dozen times before they actually die. And, although all of the great masters of all the major faiths instructed us to die before we die; I don't think this is what they had in mind.

My hunch is that they wanted us to let go of our egos. They were pointing us to the idea of letting go of our massive attempts to own and massive attempts at control. They wanted us to become at one with things and not set against things.

Death is something that we are anxious about; even when it is below the surface. In the face of that anxiety we do all sorts of weird stuff. The healthiest of the stuff we could do in light of the anxiety is to tell tales and make myths. War/murder/suicide is the unhealthiest of stuff we could do in light of the anxiety. Everything else is between these poles.

Chapter Nine

THE VEIL is thinner at night. The veil is thinner in autumn as well. That is the veil that exists between the living and the dead; between what we can see and feel and what we cannot see and cannot feel. The Celtic people called this thinning of the veil the "thin time". Things move between light and dark, life and death very freely in the "thin time". It is a time of shadows and shadow play. It is a time of movement between the sub-conscious and the conscious. It is a time of things moving up and out; or down and in.

As the sun sets, there is a force that draws back the curtain that divides reality from what we perceive. Serious images from the real meaning of life slip past the drawn curtain and enter our mundane world as the light is diminished—as its brilliance fades out to gray. The way things look and are seems to shift a bit.

When the sun is around less, people get deep and philosophic. It is probably a way of coping with the dark and our fear of the dark. If we can blather on about meaning when it is dark, then we are sure to be left alone from the evil that stalks us. We can convince ourselves there is no bogeyman.

Or, perhaps there is a different air in darkness. Perhaps the evening ether carries meaning and truth. People may be picking up signals from the deep. When the sun goes down there is a shift. There is a similar shift as summer draws to a close and we enter into autumn. You can feel this shift more dramatically than the daily one. It almost blows in one day on the wind. The light and the air become different and you just know it is fall.

Maybe people are given to intercepting one of these bits of the deep and of truth that are carried in on the darkness. They envelop it, they mull it over, and somehow they reshape it and try to share it with someone else.

Most of the time the other person that is meant to receive this fabulously reshaped truth has no clue about what is going on. They just hear the pause, see the look of satori on the others' face, and then just go all puzzled when they try to figure out where the segue was for the terribly new and mutant conversation their friend just began.

Sometimes people are not in the mood for the shift. Many times it works—mostly because of alcohol. A glass of merlot in the evening helps us to settle into the shift in meaning. We tend to be able to tolerate the shift better if we can relax into it. These shifts and deep words are important.

People make a lot of meaningful discoveries when the veil is thin. A lot of inventors pick up on the sound waves of the universe when the veil is thin. It is entrance into the cosmic dreamtime.

In the thin time between day and night people tend to be able to live the dreams they have no courage for in the daylight. I noticed this early on in life. Evening is the time for vows and dreams; hopes and decisions.

The daytime is certainly no time to have meaningful experiences and certainly not every day—all day. But, then again, we are talking about death here. As the light softens throughout the day, people turn to the existential. But, when someone enters into the dying process all of this changes. We are able to die into a newness that we may otherwise never accept.

Whether it is evening or autumn we are dying into a change. When we are entering our dying process from this life to what comes next, it is no different.

The thin time, for the dying, tends to occupy more and more of their experience. Those who are around death often experience this same type of change. Hospice workers enter into an existential landscape that is an intensified and addicting reality.

Chapter Nine

Because stability is limited in and around Death, the world of pretense may have to be inverted on occasion. As death approaches things get agitated and this means what we would normally accept as polite, normal, and appropriate behavior and standards may go by the wayside. Our new sense of normal may change on a routine basis as physical strength and focus weaken and come undone.

Life at the edge is very different from most of life we live in the center. Moving closer to death is a move toward insecurity.

All of that having been said—it does not take long to fall in love with the topsy-turvy nature of these encounters with the dance of Death—or the thinness of the veil around the dying process. Then, it is just a small stretch to get to the place where these meetings are normal. And then, it takes a few weeks of this kind of NORMAL to form an addiction to its presence—and there you have it: full scale addiction to hospice work.

After I ditched my aversion to these encounters, I began to feel the rebel. I got to be partisan to this reversal in social decorum. I learned how to use the thinness of life to help people move toward a more expanded view of themselves; a view that involved a desire to heal their inner garbage. I began to leverage the power that comes from the thin times and help patients/families to move into wholeness.

Playing devil's advocate is a role I love. I enjoyed the bravado of being able watch people open themselves to life's mystery during the day. Just like getting to see several plays—off Broadway—everyday. Stuff that was reserved in life for the thin time of evening or autumn was showing up each and every day as I worked with the dying. This meant that I had to become capable of daily change and healing myself. I needed to remain pliable enough to support the supple growth that comes with dying. I grew immensely during these encounters.

Immersed in the "art" of people's lives, I began to notice that this draining and demanding profession might actually be ennobling and transforming. I felt I might find something I was meant to find.

Its power drew me in. Instead of being sapped of energy, it expanded within me, opening to larger vistas of my own personality and capabilities.

Chapter Ten

A LARGE part of what goes on around death and dying is about helplessness. We tend to lose control over things in the process of getting closer to death. Our ability to walk is hampered, our ability to focus will shift and wane, we may lose interest in eating. The overall structure of the process is to move from fullness of life and activity to a complete cessation of life and activity, with varying degrees of decline toward that end in between.

Death is what all of the helplessness puts us on to—forces us to look at. Death leads us to helplessness; and helplessness leads us to Death. Around and around we go. And, whether it is Death the being or the death the act it does not matter. Feelings of helplessness get us to it.

The helplessness is not just going on for the person that is dying. The helplessness is going on for the intimate circle of family and friends that surround the dying. They feel helpless to be able to effectuate a change in the persons living and dying. They feel helpless at being able to effectuate a change in their own response to that person's living and dying.

The image of Ruth sitting on the edge of her sofa comes to mind—another patient. She was thoroughly wracked with pain. She had not eaten in days. She had not slept. Death had her reeling. She was gripped with the agitation that comes from dying. She could not rest. The pain had pushed her outside of herself; beyond her own self.

She sat there, undone and rattling off countless stories from her life. None of them was in any order, and none of them was completely told.

She would start with her aunt Harriet and the time they went to the circus and that telling would end with her grandmother Rose and the canning of peaches that she did; using fresh peaches from the fields outback. Then she would jump to another person and a whole new telling of a tale, which would end somewhere else and with someone else. It was a sort of story roulette.

She was also plagued with an itching and picking that seemed consuming. She would scratch or touch certain areas of her face over and over again in an unstoppable rhythm. It was clear that this tick-like movement was beyond her control or cognition. This is common and is called terminal agitation or terminal restlessness. It is treatable with both medication and therapeutic exploration.

It is pitiful to see some of the things that Death makes us go through before we can go with him. It seems like an ultimate humiliation to those who love the dying. But, scratch that surface a bit and there is a beauty there too. If you can begin to learn what is going on and figure out the antidote to these disturbances, death can provide so much growth.

I guess that is the difficulty of this whole myth—death is a separation (somehow) from everything we have known up until this point. Although Death is taking us away from all we have bonded to, there seems to be a beauty in being separated.

It is during this separation process we recognize—with a gasp—that each thing we grew close to was a rare gift of awe and splendor. Everything we have connected to or participated with in life is somehow a part of us and vital to our growth. Every story is still in there and can come out. And, when it comes out it reveals a piece of who we are.

A lot of times I found people working through their lives in a backward fashion. When we would first get together, we would

Chapter Ten

talk about the here and now life. But, as we spent time together, we would begin to speak about things that had happened a while ago in their lives. Then, we would get to a place where we would talk about things that happened a long time ago—in their earliest known days of life.

If I was working with people that grew up in the old country or in another culture, another layer was added to the mix. As we got further into uncovering their life drama—as we got further back—it was not uncommon for people who spoke a second language (a language from the first half of their lives) to revert back to that language as they approached the end. That took me by surprise.

In essence it is an unwinding of the life lived. It is like watching the video rewind while it is on play. Things move backward, slowly and somewhat out of sequence. But you can still notice the splendor of the events portrayed. There is a missing of the events that begins to grow inside when you see them flash by. A sweet sorrow is surely the right term.

Ruth went on and on and on until she was so worn out she could not stay awake. She crashed. And in those few hours of respite for Ruth and her children, she was able to sleep and gain composure.

One of the things that came out of her anxious rant was about a family member that had ostracized her in life. She was on the outside of the circle in her husbands' family—they never really accepted her. I went back to this issue when she awoke.

As we began to unfold the drama of this angst and turmoil in the family she began to become more comfortable and less agitated. This took place slowly over several sessions. What was so amazing was that when she finally arrived at a place of being able to express her anger at this person (who was now dead) she was also able to express that she would have no problem telling this relative how much she had hurt her (when she met up with her in the afterlife).

73

When this healing self- disclosure had run its course, Ruth was able to live calmly and peacefully for the remainder of her days. She died without agitation. The odd thing is, she had been on a large dose of medication to treat her restlessness and agitation. It had not worked. It was as if she had to remove the mitigating circumstances in her life before the medication was allowed to give her rest. She actually ended up coming off the medicine after she disclosed her inner turmoil.

Those things exist in all of us. Each one of us has piles of repressed garbage that needs to come up and out of us in order for us to be at peace in life. The issues change throughout our lives. Clearing out the garbage is so critical in attempting to live a healthy, balanced life.

We really become out of control when we plumb further into life. The people that never go below the surface do not allow themselves or others to recognize this fact. But, scratch the surface and you will see that there is very little that holds it all together. That is why so few people decide to slow down and live with any mention of contemplation. People hate silence because this stuff starts to bubble up into our view. Just like Ruth, we all have untold stories reeling below the surface. We tend to fear their escape.

Many people have left meditation aside because of the chasm of empty chatter and chaos that exists below the surface. Before true stillness can be found, you have to pierce through the intense turmoil, commotion and pandemonium that is just past the business of mundane life. Sit still, close your eyes, focus and then be transfixed by the demons.

Ruth only died a peaceful death after the turmoil overflowed and we found the source of it all and dealt with it. The process of dying is about this kind of "setting your house in order". There is so much to do and so much to see at death, but if we do not have stories about death and mythologies to show us what can go on, we will never strive for meaningful death.

Chapter Ten

~ ~ ~

Tibetan Buddhist iconography is filled with wild and ferocious images of demons and devils. These horrifying monsters that fill the statuesque pantheon of divine characters are really representations of the horrors and loves we experience in life. The attractions, desires, hopes, and aspirations we develop in life often consume us like these hungry monsters of mythology. They may also equally give us aid and respite, too. When our attractions, desires, hopes, and aspirations give us respite, they are seen as angelic or divine beings of light.

Mythology is built on these types of poles. We all have good and evil deep within us that can emerge as angelic or demonic realities. They myths are attached to the stories of the lives we have lived and our ability to relate these stories and resolve their issues. The life we live becomes the mythology of our own ability to mend and grow.

These beasts pounce on us—enter our consciousness—when we slow down and look below the surface. They become horrific when we realize that we are beginning to be pulled apart them.

These creatures are what we uncover as we approach the end of life and living. The heralds of Death are there to remind us that everything comes undone; but, we won't see them if we keep moving.

What makes many of them horrifying is recognizing how we were attached to them and dependent on them to live our lives. Seeing them depart or begin to fade before we have become resolved about them horrifies us to sadness.

The Tibetan Buddhist tradition has a wonderful and powerful mythology surrounding the orientation we grow into as death approaches. We go through a series of phases or bardos that help us get ready for the final letting go. In its fullest practice, one has a practitioner whisper these stages into our ear as we die.

The process of the bardos that emerges at death (from the teachings about listening of the Tibetan Book of the Dead) is a process of reminding the dead to listen and not be alarmed by these manifestations that bubble up from within. These images are not unusual. These images are manifestations of standard emotions, thoughts and disturbances from everyday life. If the deceased had been a meditator, they would be familiar with these visitors.

"Now listen, and do not be alarmed…" is the beginning of many of the teachings spoken into the ear of the dying and the dead. It is a way of interpreting the unfolding transformation that exists at death and the approach of death.

Do not be alarmed because you have been dealing with these things all of your life. You have been experiencing these emotions, fears, and thoughts all of your life. If you had looked inside during your distress, you would have seen them then.

Slowly, bit-by-bit, pieces of life drop away. Our notions, our ideas, our feelings and beliefs, our capabilities and activities fade one by one and we are left somewhat diminished. These changes and losses make impressions. Facing these changes and alterations a little at a time, throughout life, tends to lessen the distress that emerges when death is immanent.

We will have faced pieces of it in the past and it will not be strange to us. We will have seen the demons in many places. We will recognize the monsters. We will hold within the notion that we have dealt with these beasts in the past and they have no power here—except that which we give them.

In reality all "good and bad" seem horrifying as we see them being pulled away from us. The horror is the separation and the facing of ultimate aloneness, not the thing itself. Surely it was heaven when we were attached to the things we loved.

"Listen, and do not be alarmed . . . ."

The Tibetan Buddhists have remained supple and flexible in their understanding of death. They have realized that as we die (and in their view even after the actual death) we are reviewing our life.

Chapter Ten

We are seeing the dissolution of the countless pieces of who we have been. We remember stuff from the beginning of our days and we try to process it or figure out where it fits into who we are.

Hospice has plugged into this same understanding. Hospice teaches that as we approach the end of our lives, we need to review our lives. We need to see where the pieces fit together. And, as the Tibetan's have realized, we need to have this whispered into our ear. We may need help in seeing that the pieces do fit together and how that can come about. It would be really great if our families could help us do this; if our families could coach us into death. But, we do not have a mythology that helps them do this. Our mythology tells us that they are going through their own "stuff" surrounding our death.

We need coaches from the outside. Hospice provides these in our social myth.

"Listen, and do not be alarmed . . . ."

Chapter Eleven

ONE OF the things that I noticed changing in Dad was his ability to focus and or to control his focus. He became unable to focus on anything other than his own body and his own ailments. Even that was simply a short lived obsession on this ailment and then another short lived obsession on another ailment and then another.

The rest of the world ceased to exist. We could begin a conversation about a garden, or a soffit I was painting, but we always came back to his prostate, his knee, his feet, or his weight.

What I know about that now is that he was horrified by what he saw. Like the child that cannot stop talking about his nightmare, my father could not stop talking about his nightmare. Perhaps he felt he could unlock the power that these demons had on him by talking about them.

The talk became obsession and there was no key in his pockets that could unlock the antidote for that disease. On and on and on—looping around and around in a circle of horror, he told his same list of tales again and again. A lot like Ruth in my hospice experience.

He was transfixed by his own fears. He could not stop looking at them. He was living the bardos before he died. But, in his astonishment at the direction his life had taken, he could find no acceptance of his own fate. He could not grow into his diminishment. He believed too much in his own existence.

Or, perhaps it was the same as with the horrifying beasts. Could it have been that his obsession with these things was an acknowledgement of their being separated from him. Since this

Chapter Eleven

separation did not happen all at once it was prolonged—like these leave-takings he was living through.

One by one the horrors were paraded in front of him as they were taken away. As they were removed they flashed before him. They were like a ticker-tape parade—a grand spectacle.

I found it surprising to find out how much of the world was actually connected to my Dad's existence. Or, I should say, how much Dad thought everything was connected to him and his ailments.

It was as if he had been the great vortex of the universe. Bring up any topic and it would somehow filter itself through my father's prostate. No wonder the damned thing hurt. Bring up any other topic and he would get back around to his heart. Another would lead him into talking about his feet.

It was sad to see that the only place he felt comfortable was in his suffering. He had grown so attached to the horror of his life that its awful gaze transfixed him. He could not break the charm and spell.

He needed a coach to help him process these things; a coach that was not his son. He could not find one, nor could he allow anyone in close enough to be one. He eventually won in the battle to take his own life (he had tried at least a half a dozen times). He was the one that got away for me. He is the one that healed me into knowing what my wound was.

What was horrifying is that he had been surrounded by healthcare professionals for the last twelve years of his life. But, the system was so mismanaged that each hospitalization he started from ground zero. No one looked for the consistent thread that ran through his life. Either he was sent to a different hospital, or the newest physician never consulted with the past physician. The professionals were too busy to really listen to the family stories and piece together the progression. He fell through the cracks. I watched him fall through the cracks at the exact time that I was learning to catch people before they fell through the cracks.

DANSE MACABRE

This is important to this story because I believe one of the myths that we have actually developed in our modern age is a mythology around medicine, technology and saving our human lives over and over again. Our myth teaches that saving organic life is superior to saving the quality of "conscious" life.

I wish Dad had died when he suffered his stroke. From that day forward, he never regained the fullness of his person. He was never the same. We have failed to ask ourselves questions about the QUALITY of our myths; the QUALITY of our epic ability to save organic life.

There is the death of the hero. There is the death of our connection to myth. Saving organic life over and against the saving of the QUALITY of that life is a grave form of reductionism—a reductionism that has reduced us right out of the equation of life itself.

Watching them shoot Kennedy or watching my father drift away, where is the difference. Both were major underground shifts; one for a person and one for a culture. I mention them together because as I was watching my father unwind, I was also watching our way of life unwind. Something started to fall apart in the United States around the time someone decided it was ok to kill the president.

My father's slow demise enabled me to realize that I had seen this same pattern in our life as a nation. I saw it on a visceral and gut level. Our society was going through a massive transition and death. One that we are only beginning to identify and understand today—almost fifty years later.

Both the same, they hearken unto each other. Heroes taken away from us make us less able to hope and more inclined to look away from what is actually going on. Hence, we grab hold of denial. Whether the death is local or non-local, some of the mechanisms and coping are the same.

Chapter Eleven

I was at a place in life that I wanted to connect with my dad through his past experiences; learning to measure the length of my own days against all he had seen. I wanted to bond with him as a man. I wanted to bond with him as a father.

I wanted him to be able to bring forth tales of his journey, littered with valuable chunks of laconic wisdom that I could glean and polish for my own life's journey. Stories on how to be a man or how to be a dad would have filled the need for myth as I watched my desires for myth deteriorate.

I wanted him to tell me about when I was a kid. I wanted to tell him about how my kids were being kids, too. I wanted to know how he made it through the first few years of marriage, or fatherhood, or how he balanced his family with two jobs.

He was stuck in a place that revolved around only one story. Everything he told me about was about his pain and disintegration. Everything was about his suffering.

He was dissolving. He was dissolving with no idea of what was going on. He had never prepared for this. He had no idea that this dissolution had been coming. Because Dad had been unaware of what was coming at him, it was able to grab him by the throat.

It was a story about enduring suffering over a long period of time without the tools you have grown to use over the years to cope. You are unable to use the tools because each small brush with death took some of those tools away.

The doctors kept my Dad alive, but they never thought to wonder how this would affect him. Or, at least they never thought to mention to us that he was no longer going to be who he had been.

We need to tell stories that prepare us for this. I am telling my story to prepare you for this.

When we have brushes with death, we are changed. Those changes are not always good things.

If we would culturally value stories more, we would be better equipped to live our own. When a people stop exalting the telling of tales, they are losing their ability to interpret theirs'.

This happened in the sixties for the nation. It happened again—this time for me—when my dad died.

The attachment to his body that his broken mind took was obsessive. If he had a rash he would analyze everything to isolate it and then all medical treatments must be addressed toward the undoing of the rash.

When his legs ached, it was the same. There was nothing that was not causing this pain. He would begin by buying new sneakers. Then, he would get knee braces. Then he would seek inserts for the sneakers.

This went on and on for each infirmity. Every day was a new uncovering of things that affected other things. In essence, everything conspired to bring him down—at least in his mind; or what was left of it.

We would know he was depressed by the number of times he mentioned ointments, braces, sneakers or doctors. They all pointed to whatever ate at him.

I am still sure that if there had been some sort of healthcare system that was centrally organized around one care professional that would look at all of the disparate pieces of a persons' life and integrate the "wholeness" of their care, that we would be able to develop better outcomes for people. Dad would have been able to find the order to his stories and mend toward health like Ruth did.

I am clearly biased. I am a dreamer by nature.

Chapter Eleven

At any rate, somewhere between me trying to work things out and my father becoming more and more identified with his individual cells and pieces of his body, he succeeded in ending his traumatic tale. He walked to the road outside of his assisted living, parked his walker by the tree, took off his brand new sneakers—placing them neatly under the Velcro bag attached to his walker—and jumped in front of a cement truck.

By the time I arrived they had rushed him to the hospital. When I made it to the ER, they ushered me into the family waiting room without a word. When my sister arrived, they told us he was dead. We viewed his body and they handed me his clothes.

That was that.

That was a major brush with death that happened over a twelve year period.

"... Tap, tap and tap."

Medical technology can prolong our lives, but it has not yet learned how to offer coping to people who have lost their coping skills with each stroke, or heart-attack, or seizure. Each physical event takes a piece of us and leaves us more vulnerable to the thing that is chipping away at us.

Where are the clergy, the mythmakers, and story-tellers who can help us weave these specific events into tales that will heal us? Who will emerge to help us figure out how to take science into our lives?

That extended death process with my father scared me. That was my longest and deepest look at death. I was convinced that life is just the "dung and death" that T.S. Eliot had made poetic for us. Any of us could begin to dissolve or just plain disappear without warning—at any time—and there was nothing we could do about it.

This had been my deepest and longest look at the monsters below the surface of life. This was a major shift in my life. This was an awakening.

But there was no one around to help get me through it. No one had the words that could interpret what was going on inside. No one was there to help move the story up and out of me. I had no stories or someone whispering in my ear.

We have no such role in our society today. Not culturally. Our clergy are watered down beyond recognition. The best we can do is offer a professional position—the therapist. But, this person does not fit into the landscape of our lives like the priest or shaman. They have not known us since birth. They have not baptized and chrismated us, married and confessed us. In the demythologizing of modern society we have relegated liminal and luminal development to professionals.

My awakening is not a billable moment.

These professionals cannot fulfill the role to the depths that we require as humans. They need to be more involved. The need to have connective tissue through the whole of our lives and the drama we experience and hold as a people overtime. When clans dissolve, everything falls to hell.

Knowing what I know now, I realize that what unearths the heart in the advent of these events is not having word-power to discuss them. And, the next thing that lays you bare is when you discover the word-power to talk about this stuff, there are so few who can allow themselves to weep with you and realize the pain of living.

We long for words to describe our journey. We long for fellow journeyers to hear our tales. Even then there is a need for grace. Even with the word power to get these things out of us and into the light of day, there is no promise that we can avert our fears. Even when we weep, there is only the weeping that is its own tiring and weakening consolation.

We need to tell our tales about death. We need to be able to talk about things somewhere. We need to angst about the unstoppable nature of death. We need to lament, and love, and laugh.

Prolonging our lives with technology has kept us from having to look at that head on. We cannot stop Death. We cannot keep it at bay by not acknowledging it. Dancing with it and weeping because of it seem the only cure.

Not talking about it, or saving this talk until the final moments is clearly a fool-hearted thing to do. What if that moment should never be?

Chapter Twelve

Anyhow, I had to carry Henry back to his bed. He had tried to walk to the bedroom, but got stuck in the kitchen. He was stuck standing up, holding on to the Formica countertop. He had managed to get his boxers on.

I had actually stepped out of the room so he could attempt to dress. He had apparently gotten the boxers on and made his way to the bedroom, through the kitchen, in one and the same motion.

I had gone outside to use my cell-phone. This was before I decided that the headaches I was having were caused by the cell-phone. This was before I realized that some of our technology may be at the root of some of our confusion and destruction of our myths. A time came when I stopped using the phone. My headaches went away. But, while I still had my cell-phone, and when—on that day—I had stepped outside to use it, Henry dressed and made a dash for the bedroom.

I could have been gone a long time, and in fact I must have been, because there was nothing about Henry that could move quickly. He could only saunter or glide or drag.

When I came back in, he was frozen, and asking for some help. I carried his bone frame into his bedroom and placed it down on one of the two beds in the room.

People that die at home often live in rooms that do not look natural.

They have a bed, and then the hospice brings a bed. There is no place to store the first bed (in many cases), so there are two beds in a small one-bed room.

Chapter Twelve

People need the hospital beds so the railings keep them in and so they can be adjusted for comfort. We need to rethink some of the way we do things in order to "help" the dying.

If Henry had had two sheds, I would have jokingly called him "Henry two-sheds", but since he was dying, and since the whole bed fiasco was a healthcare system failure, it did not feel right to call him "Henry two-beds". But, every time I entered his room, the thought crossed my mind.

Friends should learn to say, "That looks horrible. There is too much clutter in that room. Frank, get that bed out of there and throw it out, or give it to Good Will, or put it in the garage. Henry is dying for gawd's sake. He doesn't need all that." It would be grand if people would just say, "Let me take that for a while." Perhaps they will learn.

When I got him in the bed we had a very long conversation about the trees in his yard. He never trusted anyone to touch the trees because they did not understand how to prune them. He did not believe anyone could take care of these pieces of his yard, of his life. I suspect he did not trust most to help take care of any piece of his life.

And so, alone at the end of his life, he was telling me he had been alone for the rest of his life. He and his trees were not understood, nor was their pruning something anyone with any intelligence could set themselves to do—correctly. He seemed to have been alone most of his life and he was clearly dying that way. One by one people and things and hobbies and passed times were being taken away.

He was telling me about his myth as he related his personal story. He was telling me that he had accepted the GREAT AMERICAN MYTH that we can just write people off because we do not like what they or doing.

After all, we do not need people. We are not all connected. We are fiercely independent. I was beginning to get the modern myth of consumerism and technology.

Eventually, the few people who had been in his life stopped coming because he was so thin and made so little sense. They became lost by his process of dying. They became so dumbfounded by what he had become that they were relieved when he was dead. Worn out like an old shoe, he was just thrown out.

This happens a lot.

We need an understanding of Death. We need to talk up a mythology of Death. We need to devise a way to speak about it that helps us get a handle on it: because, right now, our fear and ineptitude, our shameless indifference and avoidance is giving that bastard the upper hand. We need to do it in small units or clans.

They could be families. They could be religious groups. They could be neighborhoods. But somewhere, and somehow the human community needs to become familiar with its tribal roots and sit around the fires of life and discuss things deep into the evening.

We need to burn our remotes and stop simply watching stories. We need to tell stories. When we do, our stories will explain who we are; to others and most importantly to ourselves. We need to learn to weave the telling of our tales so that we can learn to weave the living of those tales.

We need to tell the tales of how things are taken away from us before we die. We lose our interest to live, our ability to walk, our desire to eat. These things will all go. Are they really as important as we pretend they are?

He comes in and snatches us away and we have no words for it. It is not that we must have words for it so we can CONTROL DEATH. We cannot do that. No, damn it, we need to have words about it so we can LIVE. We cannot live if we silently hold this critter at bay with our ignoring, head-turning glances.

Chapter Twelve

I want to laugh at him and be able to say, "I saw you coming", or, "I thought you might show up, you bastard. I was ready for you." After all, that is the best we can hope for, to have known all along that Death was there, around us, ready to strike at every turn throughout our lives, and that we lived our lives gloriously in spite of his hideous presence.

We can learn to sob about it and then to dance with Him and just keep living.

If we had a sense of Death all around us all of the time, we may allow ourselves to be more genuine. If we sensed our potential removal from life, maybe we would cherish the holding of hands and the giving of dandelions. Or other childlike acts that mean so much.

I suppose that portions of that sound a bit hostile; like I am angry at Death. I should talk about some of this.

For the most part, I would say that I do hold some anger at Death. I get mad that Death pretends to be interested in people, but is actually not. Death lulls and lures people into a dance.

But there are other pieces to my death anger. It feels to me that the larger portion of what I am angry with is the failure to recognize that Death is always dancing around us and that we should never be in denial that this breath could be our last.

I am angry that we have stopped telling stories about Death, (about life, too.) We do not hold the idea in the front of our mind. Even our religious leaders pretend that it does not exist or that we do not dread it.

Failure to see Death dancing or at least to acknowledge that story keeps us from truly living and being in the moment. All of that refusal to accept the tentative nature of life encrusts us and causes us to believe that we are owed another day. We mistakenly

DANSE MACABRE

teach ourselves to accept a sense of entitlement that we deserve another day and another chance.

Death tends to negate that entitlement.

The ease with which Death moves in and around us—quietly disturbing major portions of people's lives—is maddening. One-day people are out in the yard, planting daffodil bulbs; Death sneaks by—casually—and takes one to the ground.

Stroke. That begins that persons Dance with Death. Each day they take new steps, Death changes what used to be their rhythmic and metered life; Death teaches them to Dance the Dance that will eventually make them disappear from life.

I am mad because Death teaches us to be suspect of casual and mundane and simple joyfulness. I anger that we accept this lie. Plant a garden and enjoy it and you better watch out; It could be coming. Go to a family picnic and see all of the folks that have been absent from your eyes for the past year; It will take someone.

I am mad because there is often no warning that you are going to start the Dance Macabre. He just shows up—unannounced and unexpected—and either teaches you slowly with several sinkable episodes, or teaches you the whole damned jig all at once. And let's face it, I madden that we neglect keeping this before our eyes and we act surprised when He shows up for us. We expect an advanced notice.

There are no announcements and no invitations. And yet they are all around us. Other people drop off and disappear and we should not forget. We all go to funerals, and our lives and behaviors change for a day or two at best. We need to bring the awareness of the continual presence to the fore of our thinking, feeling, and our discussions. It is probably the greatest single event in our lives after our birth. How will we deal with it?

"Dance," the rude bastard says, to his startled acquaintance.

Chapter Thirteen

APPARENTLY, IN 1338 and well into 1339, Death showed up for a grand performance at a little village of Nestorian Christians. The village was known as Issyk-Kul, it lay south of Lake Balkhash, Russia.

The cemetery headstones made clear a major work of the macabre had taken place in that short year. Three of the stones actually told us that the THE PLAGUE killed the people buried there. It was etched into their epitaph. THE PLAGUE.

And so it began. One of Europe's largest choreographed pieces—by Death—began in a humble village and played over and over again through towns and cities until two thirds of human life within her boundaries was buried from Dancing so well with Death.

Death danced and collected a huge retinue of followers who danced along with Him. He danced two thirds of the world's population right into whatever it is that comes next. The human psyche was so marred by the alteration in its ethos that macabre art developed and flourished from that point on, showing Death as a luring and lulling character inviting people to join Him. We knew that we had to tell the tale of how fragile life really is.

First came a bite; most likely from a flea. That is how the plague begins; how Death's dance in the 14th century got its start.

Then, a few days should be allowed for the steps to be learned; for the illness to incubate. Next comes the fever; you get the shakes, you throw-up, you can't stand the light and you thrash about in pain.

DANSE MACABRE

By the time day three or four arrives, you are dancing so constantly that you begin to give in to heart failure and sheer exhaustion. But, you don't usually just die; you agonize like this for a bit, developing egg-sized lumps around your lymph-nodes. Then the internal bleeding begins. That is when you die.

We had to do something with the angst of this madness. We had to process the horror of this sort of human vulnerability.

Imagine the intense fear that grew out of the dance of Death in Europe. By the year 1421 most everyone was gone. Unannounced in a little hamlet, Death started something that we can only shiver at.

Society had to be restructured, values had to be realigned, and people—mass hordes of people—had to hide the idea that Death could do that again. Burying millions of people can only make you decide to blot out the fact that it ever happened—even the first time.

Months into the plague, the talisman makers got rich. They built places of "healing" and churches. They gilded the walls and ceilings with gold.

Clergy got rich. They built side chapels with more gold leaf. They became opulently rich and died of the plague themselves.

Then there is the aggression that arose from the repressed fear.

Because shoving something down in can only presume that at some time it will climb up and out, you can be sure that people had strong responses to the endless dying. They had responses that were not quiet and demur. People must have become monsters. Looting and pillaging were signs of a madness within. Those that did not die from the plague became dead inside—hollow men, losing hope and stability.

We are always just one village away from this kind of death. He still sneaks around, tempting people to just jiggle one foot. And we do still act as if we will never fall for His alluring Dance.

Chapter Thirteen

Listen to Gustave Flaubert's romantic ramblings from his 1838 piece, "Dance of Death."

"Each morning I depart, each evening I return, bearing within my mantle's ample folds all that my scythe has gathered. And then, I scatter them to the four winds of Heaven!

"The foaming waters cool my weary feet, burning from bathing in the falling tears of countless generations that have clung to them in vain endeavour to arrest my steps

"My horse! Ah, yes, my horse. I love thee too! How thou rushest o'er the world! Thy hooves of steel resounding on the heads bruised by thy speeding feet. Never art thou weary. Never do we rest. Never do we sleep.

"Where'er my arrows fly, thou overturnest pyramids and empires, trampling down crowns beneath thy hoofs; all men respect thee; nay, adore thee! To invoke thy favour, popes offer thee their triple crowns and kings their scepters; peoples their secret sorrows; poets, their renown. All cringe and kneel before thee, yet thou rushest on over their prostrate forms.

"But on my work must go; my path I must pursue; it leads through infinite space and all the worlds. I sweep away men's plans together with their triumphs, their loves together with their crimes, their very all.

"My eyes turn towards a glowing horizon, boundless, immense, seeming to grow increasingly in height and depth. I shall devour it, as I have devoured all else."

Not only does He show up unannounced, He is a rude pig—devouring way too much. And we, all the while collude to ignore His arrival. We agree to pretend He is busy elsewhere and not with us. How shall we stop this? Will we ever become aware that death is always in our midst? Will we wake up and tell the tales around the fire; the tales that will prepare us for the Dance of a lifetime?

Chapter Fourteen

Tragedy often strikes without any advanced warning. When it does, it can knock us clear off the ground we thought we were standing on.

In 1995 my wife and I lost a child in-utero. We had to choose to abort our 4-month in-utero daughter, after nine years of marriage, six years of concerted attempts to get pregnant, and two and a half years of fertility specialists (this means at least once a week visits...if not more). By a miracle of faith and science we had conceived; in the same instant and severe flash, we had to choose to end her life.

There were multiple birth defects: Turner's syndrome, cystic hygromas, and an exposed spine. We actually had to choose to end the pregnancy because the tumors that were surrounding Zoe Alexander's head were becoming large enough to endanger my wife, Glinda. We were not prepared for this.

Not only were we not prepared to lose this child; we were not prepared to end this child's life. We had no real idea the universe could be such a cruel and thankless place. We knew some about the universe, of her awe and amazement and beauty, but not her stinking hunger for life. And so, in the final throes of the winter 1995, my wife and I entered the descent into grief that would change our lives and the way we looked at living.

There were countless hours of grieving. Hours of tears and gut wrenching sobs. The agony came from a place deep inside, a place I really did not know existed. But, once that place had been opened up—exposed—I would never return to the place I had been before. My life, like it or not, had been transformed.

Chapter Fourteen

Grieving is a very real way of looking at life. Grieving is a longing for something that is not. Something we want that is not ours, or a part of us. We long for it, we strive, we groan, we grieve. My grieving for the separation I felt from the loss of our little girl, opened up the tears of a thousand lifetimes. The tears of every separation and loss I had ever known—a countless grieving I did not know—came to the fore of my feeling.

When I was not walking around with pained eyes and a sore stomach from sobbing, I was in a daze—numbed from the agony. In many ways I felt as if I was descending into a dungeon. With every step I took, I felt myself becoming more and more the dread and feared monster of the dark basement—Grendel of the depths. I was descending into the depths of my own self. In the descending I found grief.

Grieving cuts open the invisible veil between the body and feeling. It unleashes all sorts of feelings from the center of our being. Feelings that were being felt, but being stuffed because there were no words to express them, or words to help us learn to sit quietly in the presence of the feelings, or no safe place to feel them without being rejected and or scoffed. Grieving takes us to the bottom of the pit of anguish where it does not matter anymore if you have words, or are neglected or mocked. At the bottom of the pit you realize you are utterly alone, and nothing else is important.

I am not really sure why grieving does this, but I know it does. Perhaps it has to do with nature of loss that surrounds grieving. Grieving is about losing things. And, perhaps it has to do with the magnitude of loss. I mean, maybe we cut open the veil between the body and feeling when we have either lost so much, or lost someone really big. I don't know.

I do know grieving the loss of our Zoe Alexandra cut open the veil between my body and my feeling. That grief was the final straw. I broke down and sobbed and sobbed and sobbed. Not only did I grieve the loss of a child, but the loss of my innocence, the loss of my faith, the loss of so many things in life up until that day.

The tears and the grief, though, far from isolating me from things, opened me to feeling through things—mostly through the earth. I sensed a new connection with everything around me. And, although people who understood the path of grieving were few, it seemed all of creation knew about grieving. All creation seems to groan, as it were, anyhow. Every rock and tree and clump of moss understood my tears and stood in reverential awe at my moments of suffering. Grief can open us. It opens the body to feel. It opens the body to the earth. It opens the body to the universe.

There has been a lot of work done on grieving. Elisabeth Kubler-Ross was kind enough to share the painstaking and pioneering work she unearthed in the realm of death and dying and the subsequent grief work. Her work with the stages of denial/isolation, anger, bargaining, depression, and acceptance was and is a monument for learning to cope. But, all of the cognitive paradigms in the world are of no use when the mind is not in unison—both thought and feeling. Knowing about the stages is useless, unless we are able to open up to the feelings that portray the thoughts.

There is a real deficit in the world today. That deficit is in the arena of living in the heart. Many people live in their "minds". Actually the place where these people live is in the head. The head is the place of thoughts and ideas. It is a safe place. It is a place where we can make up the rules, the morals, the ethics, and the outcomes. But, it is not the place of presence. The heart is the place of presence. The heart is where we live out what we are truly capable of.

We have all known people with high ideals and moral structures. Many of them do not feel the way they think. They exist in two separate places. In reality, however, the heart and the feelings of the heart are a part of the mind. And, although this view has fallen from understanding today, this does not mean it is not a reality. The heart is within the mind, and so is the brain. It is both thinking and feeling that make up the human mind.

Chapter Fourteen

When these two streams come together and merge, then a person is capable of great things. Then a person is capable of being truly present, accepting and compassionate.

In the process of bringing our ideas about grief and our feelings of grief together, we must be about a great work. This great work may take the form of art, or it may take the form of activity, it may take the form of silence, or it may take the form of therapy. This great work will be to merge the feelings of the heart with the thoughts of the brain. As we express the feelings and thoughts together, and as we pass through time, integration will occur and a new life will be fashioned. This new life will now include the ideas and feelings of loss and separation, of impermanence and suffering, of grief and death.

For each individual it will be a different process in terms of its length and its shape, but what will not be different is that each person must go through it. Each person must feel and think, and then express those feelings and thinking over time. If they are held onto, integration will not be complete.

There are many large feelings that I remember from the process. There is being lost, surrounded, engulfed, dirty, wet, dark, moist, empty, numb, voiceless, dead, alone, abandoned. On and on goes the list. I tried to express exactly what I was feeling, whether it seemed to make logical sense or not. I tried to give voice to my heart.

As I gave voice to my heart, I felt the rest of me shift into place. I became unified if you will. My brain did not have its usual need for controlling my feelings, it just watched them. This whole process sponsored a larger feeling in me, that feeling was surprise/awe. I was amazed at the depth of my own character and identity. The feelings that emerged from me, made me unsure of my own beginning and ending. I felt I had another whole person inside, one that very rarely came out to play. This person had completely different views and perspectives than I was used to.

DANSE MACABRE

I found that I could no longer accept a typical view of an individual God who rules the earth and the cosmos from His point of view—which is utterly random for the creatures He has made. No, that didn't work.

Grieving destroys patriarchal images of God—the images of God as supreme Father-Ruler—and opens the body to the heart as the seat of God. It opens the body to suffering and the great pathos that flows through all living beings below the surface of numbed skin. Grieving opens us to the Divine Mother image of God. The image of the eternal feminine that monthly travails in wombic pain. The image of stayed and steady consistent nurturance, even through travail. This is not to say that there is no masculine aspect to whatever the divine is. It is to say that the child tends to start there—with the view of God as a protecting daddy—but will move beyond that some day if he or she feels the terribly wild sting of loss. Loss and grief are ferociously random feelings. They come from a place in us that is connected to continual suffering.

Grieving put me in touch with a deeper level of feeling. That is what these poems are about. Not all of them are about our tragic loss of Zoe Alexandra, but they all show the attention of inner grief. Some are about grieving in general, experiencing loss. They are in no way about trying to offer an answer to suffering. They are about feeling suffering—feeling death and loss. They are about feeling the shift of loss, death, and grief.

May the poems open you and give you peace in knowing that others feel separation and loss deeply—as do you.

∽ ∽ ∽

These are my tales for you—my myths—of how death ravished my life and came in to rule me for a season. These are my personal stories of how one death impacted me.

These are what has come up and out of me.

THE ZOE ALEXANDRA POEMS

DANSE MACABRE

One Second

It only takes one second
for the soul to leave the body.
A flicker on the screen,
a tightening of the face
and it drains right out.
From the head-
through the heart-
out of the feet-
onto the highly polished
gray flecked white
linoleum floor.
And the pathways of ecstasy
become vacant,
the heart becomes hollow,
and the mind numbed
becomes one-pointedly empty.
Gone;
hope,
joy,
elation.
It only takes one second
for the soul to leave the body.

Chapter Fourteen

Zoe

That she was born to us in
mottled hues is known.
We did not want to have
her sucked out of the womb
into disparate death. But, the
cry came over the mountain,
and it spoke of war and bloodshed.
We had set ourselves to killing
God. We wanted to route Him out;
for, He had shammed us; toyed with
all that we had done that had been
good. We fought Him hard. But He
was everywhere and we lost strength.
The tolls could not be
measured accurately.
How much damage
had we done? How many
limbs had He lost?
Mist settled into our days
and the battling ceased
to the haunting sound of
the loons on the water.
We had only one casualty.
When she left, she took our
souls. She held them like
parcels, or books under
her arms as she swam in
the vast and forever blue sea.
She has sent back pieces of
them. For us. She pulls off
something from here, something
from there, and floats it in on

DANSE MACABRE

    the surface of the cold
    churning waves. It will come
    in as a petal, or a moss. It
    will come in as a tear, or the
    sound of the pipes over the
    Highlands.
    Was there not some deep
    settling as I crossed the path
    exposed by the tide, to touch the
    the heather. There is the heather.

Chapter Fourteen

Gathering

I have been away for a while;
out gathering in the fields.
I have pulled up lots of good
stuff, by the roots, and have
put them in my basket over
my shoulder—the basket at my side.
I have been away from myself
collecting new foods, new stuff for
the journey. Having just gotten
back, I now know I was gone.
I am happy to be back, because now
I can begin again to bake the bread,
and light the candles, to draw the
bath and to work the poems, to be
about the things I laid aside so I
could gather new foods; bring in new
stuff. This feeling is as refreshing and
surrounding as the two feet of snow,
drifting this way and that outside of
my home, outside of me.

DANSE MACABRE

A Loon Cries

There is a deep sadness,
like a cello in the heart
that plays, and plays, and
plays itself out—
a river of tears
and woes
without end.
There is a note of sadness
even in the most
joyous moment.
It is all that distance. It
is the sadness of moving
away—of separation.
It is the recognition of
contraction, of making
the invisible
visible.
A loon cries and wails
its call of love across
the surface of the waters and
we, somehow, cock our heads
to the side and feel the
space open in the top
of our heart and we feel
a sad joy. The water there
is dark and the moon, the
moon is bright and full.

A Man's Grief

A man's grief is
somehow different.
It starts from separation.
He is not the same as
all other things. He really
does not feel like an ocean
or a great body of water.
There is a difference.
He is not the same as the
mother who gave
him all that he became. From
the start he knows he is the
OTHER.
He is not the same
as all other things. This makes
a man stand one step back.
This is his grieving. Not as close
to it, to anything, as he
might imagine he could be.
There is a hole in him,
in man. It is there to
mimic the womb. But it
is bottomless.
This hole drops endlessly down.
A man falls into this hole—this
hole of his—at some point.
When he is
not really looking.
Maybe he can fill the hole,
by screwing everything
in sight, by taking control
over all that he can touch.
Maybe if he fills other things

DANSE MACABRE

with himself, he will somehow
fill the emptiness of the hole.
Standing,
one step back,
he can only approach
the edge
so far.
There he stands,
feet firmly planted on the
ground, staring into the sea.
The endless sea.
Grieving.
And that day
is the day the hole is filled.

Chapter Fourteen

As Humans Grieve —for Robert Bly

I did not know
what he meant
when he said,
"he has not grieved
as humans grieve."
But now, I feel
his meaning all throughout me,
all over the place.
Grief has a cadence;
a beating of the wing
with honk,
as the flock moves,
slowly,
a line in the distance,
over the nearby pond.
This character that grieves,
This one inside, he has
his back against the
Stucco wall and his ass
is seated on the marble bench.
The brown leaves blow loudly
about his feet, in the crow-cold
winds and purpling-gray skies.
Only just now has he learned
he will not fall forever into
the pit at his side.
The walls of the pit
fly by him—up, always up—
he grieves.
This one inside has only
Just begun to grieve. In his
Beginning he grieves like

DANSE MACABRE

an animal. A howling dog.
Twisting, twirling,
Unleashed, undone
he has no other
place to go but to the den
of tears and ash,
of sweat and blood, down,
down, down
at the bottom of the pit.
In his howling and falling he changes.
Passing through silence into anguish
He emerges someone new.
He is a man now. He has recovered
a bit from the tortured side. He has some
silence in the night. He has some loss.
His eyes, sore from
sobbing, are covered by dark glasses;
his appearance is disheveled and unkempt.
But he sits there, on his bench.
An animal, become a man.
He is different. But he does not say
wiser. He does not believe, anymore,
that the answer is in his hand, or in his
reach, or even out there—at all. He knows
it is a matter of time before the bench
slides over, and again he falls into the pit, and
again he becomes an animal. A man no more.
For now,
until then,
he is a god.
Gods sit in silence,
on their benches,
and they wait.
Gods are what

Chapter Fourteen

we are when
we are not animals.
Gods feel and know
something about
the crazy cycles
that keep pushing us
to the edge and
over the edge.
He sits there,
on his ass,
with his sore eyes,
and is a god. For just
a little bit. A god who
wept there, in confusion—
somewhere between
compost and glory.
That is how
 a human grieves.

DANSE MACABRE

INTO THE EARTH

Snow melts
into the earth,
and dirt swells
gladly
holding it
for the sun's passing.
Drinking from
these
fresh streams
can only come
by dying.

IN THE WAITING

In the waiting
when the mouth can only
open to the throat
and croak curses—
the heart prays in silence.
Her frail thin,
dandelion-stem limbs
turn and pull.
Clutching her head
she wriggles, trapped
in the tunnel of my
wife's flesh,
unable to know
the mass hanging
on her skull
keeping her a freak on
her way to choking.
What will be?

Chapter Fourteen

Elixir

I know what the silver
elixir was.
The drink I stole and
consumed to slake
my thirst.
It was grief;
and O how it
burned out my soul
and ran through my body,
out of my toes,
onto my sandals.
It came to me
A week ago in a dream
posing as a drink
I was told I should not
drink.
O mercurial elixir,
O burning change.
I know what the silver elixir was.
It was Zoe and the alchemy of
hellish change that has begun.

DANSE MACABRE

Untouched Fingers

Untouched fingers.
Ribbons of flesh
wrapped around a tender
unknown face.
My child,
 Zoe,
"Good-Bye."
The words I used so
easily, have taken on
a new emptiness.
The pain is so deep
it is ecstasy
and I am numb.
I can only feel you
being torn away.
I will
not hold your untouched
fingers. They will be
taken away.

Chapter Fourteen

Moon Rays

I looked for the strong
rays of the moon
the night we anointed
you with myrrh.
Even a soft glow would
have given me strength.
There was no moon—
there was no strength.
I wanted to tell you how
beautiful the moon is:
how she is full of energy
for the dark side
for the soft side.
I remember first seeing
your arms—fresh dandelion
stems moving—moving
about your sides.
You brought us such joy.
I wanted to walk with
you in the daffodil
fields by our first home,
teach you how to hold
a butterfly on your
finger, and let
you eat clover with
the rabbits.
The tea we would have had,
made with peppermint leaves
from our garden,
would have made you smile—
feeling its tingle and honeyed
sweetness in your mouth.

DANSE MACABRE

Hand in hand we would
have walked the sands
while the mother-waters
crashed on the beach and
the sun put itself to bed—
glowing ourselves
with a powerful peace
and cheer.
I want you to stay with us,
Zoe Alexandra,
and join our circle
as we taste the earth,
touch beauty, and dance through
separating pains.

Chapter Fourteen

Tear Clouds

The clouds held rain
like our tears—
heavy beyond holding.
For days they spilled
out of our eyes,
over our lids,
down our cheeks
in unending streams of warmth.
O God,
how,
even when we had stopped
crying, how they did run
out, slopping over the sides
of our bucketed hearts.
Never-ending.
I cannot
form the questions.
The mind has ceased
and the heart has
joined forces with
the body.
The mind's grief is confusion.
Its grief is not the grief of
the rest of the body—
those wrenching, twisted
knotted aches.
It is more
a still grief.
Unsure and childish.
The body mourns and mourns
and mourns, becoming empty
and endlessly full,

DANSE MACABRE

    changing the course
    of life—
    Never to be the same again.
    The mind grieves confusion.
    The heart holds hands with the
    body and pours out its grief
    onto the rutted
    earth that is grooved
    by the soul of time forever.
    Weather changing deeply,
    clouds moving endlessly to the
    rhythm of drenching and drying;
    digging trenches in soft feeling
    that screams in pain.

Chapter Fourteen

Thousands of Years of Staring

The smell of wood
burning in the fireplace
dances in the air
mixing with the
sound of the river.
Today, I am sure
we learned about motion
by watching the water.
Thousands of years of staring,
daily staring,
heavy staring,
into the flowing
wetness –
driven moisture –
made them sure they
could float a log
or turn a wheel.
I have come here for
the sound of her movement,
for the peace of
her traveling—to hide from
Zoe's death.
The geese come here.
They move at sunset..
as the glow disappears,
a chorus swells.
One goose
carries the point of
the song;
pounding home the call
to make music.
"Sing. Sing," she calls.

DANSE MACABRE

And, they do.
A lovely song.
It grows and deepens
as they approach.
And, as they are overhead,
I close my eyes, and
with Rumi, I raise my
hand and drink in
the secret nectar.
I dance.
Twirl,
pause,
slide, whirl.
I have come here
for the geese.
I have come here
for them to sing
the song for me.
This past week
our little girl died.
Zoe Alexander,
laden with cysts on
her head and spine,
died inside her mother.
We saw her on the
screen. Little hands and feet.
A cord, and cysts. Before
they could take her from us,
she died.
I came to the river to
stare. My numbness screams
out to listen. I came here to
hear the geese. Here
there are no words of consolation,

Chapter Fourteen

no words of hope; but,
the pounding of the silence
and the movement.
I came to the river
that the one goose might carry
the point of the song for me.
For now, I must stare, and feel
the pounding rhythm of darkling flow
within my arches, within my chest.

DANSE MACABRE

Mingled

It is coming up through me
from the ground.
My feet are pulling it
out of the earth—
tearing it
from the dirt.
It is dark,
silvery,
heavy and full
of power.
My heart beats with it
these days.
It courses through
all my veins—
ivory growing from bone
and iron deposits in the
hot and cooling core.
It bubbles.
There is no joy
in this grief
that comes from
the dirt,
that comes from
the ground
and from death.
There is rest
sometimes,
but there is no joy.
It mingles with me
and falls down again.
Trying to pull me
back in to its depths.

Chapter Fourteen

I pull to keep myself
from going in,
from going under.
My pulling
and its
pulling get
lost and mixed
together and
unclear. Who is
pulling which and
which whom?
Traces of silvery pools
mix with blood and seep
into the crevices of
the cracked dirt.
No tree will grow here,
no blade of grass.
Only the buzzards
will come
and peck at the soil;
tasting for death
between the broken
earth and the pieces
of bloodied gravel.

DANSE MACABRE

A Bell

Few people hear
me when I say,
"I hate God for
killing our baby."
It is not
that I whisper.
They turn deaf ears,
because hearing those
words would bring them
death or abomination.
A leper turned out from
his parents' home.
And yet I say them.
The bell rings clearly as
the fog envelopes its cold,
rusted metal—a buoy
heaving in the purple gray
chunks of water
that rise and fall.
They do not feel
this hollow aching deadness.
I do.
Have they never felt it?
Why?
I have had inklings of it
all along. It deepens.
Takes more flesh each
time it comes near.
A succubus writhing on
me; and at once,
clawing, gouges at my eyes
and heart.

Chapter Fourteen

And if He did not kill
our girl,
He did not wave His hand
to bless her and make her well.
This I cannot forgive.
No, whatever He did or
did not do
killed our daughter. And,
we had to choose to end it all.
The limb broke off
and tore through the roof.
We are left to clean up the mess.
The wind is gone and we are left.
It hurts. Oh God, how it hurts.

DANSE MACABRE

Hardening

The heart has wounds all around it.
Places where arrows once
tore and bloodied muscle.
They have healed since then,
turning gray-brown, flat
not giving or returning
when poked with a finger.
Some trees turn to stone.
A curious thing. They
just up and become some
other thing. They become
something else.
Pieces
of me have turned to stone.
The dead pieces.
Mostly the wounds
around the heart.
There are other place too,
just below my ass, where
I used to welt up after
a belting. That turned to
pine and then
to stone. My little toe
is still turning from wood
to stone. I don't know why,
but it is all twisted—all
humped up. It is becoming
a statue.
At times
I feel the top of my
back—the field between
my shoulders—hunching up.
A swelling mountain

Chapter Fourteen

pushing through the skin.
That one I think I'll stop.
But who knows.
Trees that turn to stone
are a curious thing.
The body has dead men
all around it. People who
have once lived,
or maybe not.
They walked with me
and I have spoken
with them, but the hollow
behind their eyes would
not let them raise a fist
and yell with me. They
softened. They became
jelly.
At some point,
when I was not looking—
or maybe I was—
the hand and the fist
crumbled, the jelly glued
shut the lid. No more air
could enter; and they
too were stone.
Can anything stop this
constant turning of things
into stone?
This turning to stone
is a curious thing.

DANSE MACABRE

No Myth

What happens when
myths stop coming up
out of the ground?
A great fire-bird does not
come out of the traveling sun.
A crane no longer hangs
above the lake.
A clump of growth that
hangs over a crack in the
cement is a weed.
Extracted from the earth
is a story, the heart
has no place.
Wandering,
the spirits are wandering.
The microscope gives us
our answer and the camera
removes all doubt.
There is nothing to tell
around the fire, but
random tragedies,
rampant destructions,
fascinating facts.
Dissolve imagination,
shut out dreams,
stop making tales.
There is no need for poems,
or for stories, or for the making
of myths.
Community is gone
and woven tales are no longer
permitted to come out
of the earth.

Chapter Fourteen

EMPTY

There is an emptiness in me
that cannot form words
or even hear them.
A crack in the macadam
with not even a weed—
unwanted thing—
poking through to the sun.
It may be because our
child is now dead;
or because this is the
time in the mottled and damp
green-brown world
for no stirrings.
Nothing moves but birds
on the top, scouring
the moist earth for worms
to pull up from the dirt.
Scabs from the skin.
Pre-spring death just hangs
dank,
blends with silhouettes
and with the ground
and just stays there.
Slowly. Slowly the birds
will bring back the daffodil's
yellow, the tulip's red, and
the skies lion blue.
Slowly
the crocus will push up,
burst and fade to milky
white. When this has come,
perhaps by then, words
will return. Words that feel
as if they have meaning.

DANSE MACABRE

No Relief

There is no relief here.
Nothing around me brings
solace or joyful comfort.
There is no relief.
The grasses lay dormant—
muddied and clumped in
cold dampness—
they wait.
Warmth will come
and the birds will not recognize
the new terrain of
pleasant growth and greenness.
Their talons will no longer push
their way into the mud,
but will lay flat
on the earth's firmness.
We lost our daughter.
Zoe is dead.
How can this have happened.
A piece in us that was
growing hope has
been torn out.
Does she walk the muddied
earth or climb the rocks
strewn with amber mosses?
Does she know the rented pain
we pay for?
How can we go on?
The love my love holds
for me is empty—there is no
solace there, there
is no calm.

Chapter Fourteen

She holds an empty shell
encrusted with a painful
residue of hope. Gone.
O God, how long?

DANSE MACABRE

One Year

Last year
at this same time
we were packing
to go to Greece.
The islands of
honey and stone
left the ocean, and basil, and
olives in our soul.
Tinos held the smell
of warm sun—
baked chamomile, growing
between the earth and
veins of green marble.
Aegina, the shaded home
of olive orchards
and cyprus trees.
And now,
now I am cut in
half with pain.
O Virgin,
O Nectarios,
what has happened?
Who chose to blow our
world apart and steal
our little girl-gift
from Glinda's womb.
Who did not choose—
did not choose to help.
All I see
passing before the eyes of
my heart are
the churches,
the seaside,

Chapter Fourteen

the taverns,
and the tired
worn people of the
earth; of the faith.
How happy we were;
how full of joy, and
oil and wine and mirth.
How dry our hearts were;
dry of tears and filled with
laughter and sex.
That joy,
that joy now
lets me weep;
cuts me in half to weep.
Grieving,
grieving,
grief.
The harrowing beauty of
the small hearty flowers and
strong gnarly herbs of that
place, and our joy
lets me,
no,
makes me weep.

DANSE MACABRE

Broken Waters

He who stands
upon the precipice
and stares
into the dimpled waters—
broken and moved by the wind—
He,
he shall emerge
from the deep
with his sword clenched
tightly in his teeth.
He shall fight
and he shall win.
He is of the earth
and he is of the deep,
and he is of
his own Self.
He not only stares
into the waters;
He sees.

Chapter Fourteen

Yellow

The pain is still here,
but the daffodils
have begun to bloom.
If there must be pain,
it should be felt amid beauty;
amid soft and gentle folds
of flower flesh
and buzzing bees.

DANSE MACABRE

Feeling the Earth

Once you reach
your hand down
into the earth,
pushing it in, up to the
elbow,
it is hard to see
what you're
after.
Even if
you could
somehow
pull yourself in—
with that submerged arm—
it would be hard
to see
in the dirt.
The earth
is about feeling.
Sensing a movement
out of
the corner of the eye
is for above ground.
The dirt is about feeling,
about damp movements
within.

Chapter Fourteen

Feeling a shift, a
dark inner sense,
there is no word,
no thought; only the
damp, dank scent
of wetness and
dried parched earth.
Feeling the earth is
all there is to grieving.

DANSE MACABRE

GRIEVING REQUIRES A HAND

I have grieved enough to
know youth has ended.
Now I am a man.
The tree no longer just
dies, but I must take it
down and stack it neatly
or cut it or find some
place to drag it or burn it.
No one helps me bury the rabbit.
When I open the cage and there
is no movement, no advance
toward the clover I bring, it is me
that digs the hole and worries
if it is deep enough.
I ask, "When should my grieving
stop. How long is too long?"
The herbs need pruning.
A man knows this.
It is why he stays.
Grieving requires a hand,
it works on the tree.
A piece is trimmed,
a branch is cut, to be
burned, buried, or
scattered, or sometimes
brought into the house.
Grieving requires a hand.
Leaves that stay too long
on the ground do not get
raked. They lump up and
mottle and take their own place.
Grass, for a season,

can only push around them
and not through.
In the numbing,
the hand is stilled.
A man feels less than
human. A thing.
A mottle and a lump of
feeling; too big
to be moved.
The snow melts on the warm
drive and flows into ice—
untouched by the push of
an arm and a shovel.
A sometime rock it stays,
and the man goes.
Sliding on the top
of the waters,
a man wonders what
happened to the lake
he fished dry.
Will the sunnies return—
come back here—or,
are they there,
down there,
frozen in the mud.
He tries to thaw them
with the breath of his memories,
but he cannot.
And,
if he did,
he would fall in
and flounder
and become what he
once fished for—

DANSE MACABRE

frozen in the mud.
He stands,
and for now,
can only wonder.
This is why he stays.
The sun lights the
earth from behind
the gray and snow-filled
pall. The jay pushes through
the drift to find a seed
that may or may not
still be there.

Chapter Fourteen

HE SITS THERE

He sits there—
his lips together,
so tightly,
turning red with anger,
and, he denies he is
upset.
He says he does not understand;
and, he is damned straight he
does not understand
He knows nothing of
the gut wrenching
pain that cuts us
in half at having to have
our baby killed.
And then,
he can show up with
food and flowers, smiling
while he is working to take
my wife's job;
smiling while she is
grieving.
He still believes in
a God, and does not raise a
fist at Him—sharing my anger.
He is damned straight he
does not understand.
I cannot believe the distance that
has grown into
our lives—into our
friendship.

DANSE MACABRE

A Soft Flute

A soft flute
and a gentle
blowing of the chimes
has sneaked
into my anguish
and brought a
familiar wash of peace.
Days have passed,
many days
since that feeling
has found a home
in me.
I was glad
it came to me,
if only
for a moment.
Came to me on the sound
of a soft flute on the air.

Chapter Fourteen

Understanding

So many thoughts and
so many words
pass across this dirt.
A middle-aged woman
tells her friend that she
is only kidding, only
teasing, but
does her friend understand—
she, in her twenties,
retarded,
drooling,
her meal spread out
across her too small shirt,
across the too small booth
in the dimly lit Italian restaurant.
A father reaches out his hand
to his son, telling him, as they walk,
they cannot afford to buy too much—
since he lost his job. The child looks
up into his father's eyes and says he
only wants a candy bar.
The bulbs spend all their strength,
all their energy to push their stalky
greens up through the hard and
thawing dirt. The winds howl and
bring cold; and the frost kills the
flowers and the hard-tight blooms.
I have set my sight
toward the horizon,
toward the sinking
fireball, and I walk.
I do not understand why
my heart has left me, or why

DANSE MACABRE

a sudden questioning
has interrupted my walk. It is the Loss.
How could we have been singled
out to bear a monster? How could
we have been chosen to be the
ones to have to choose to kill
our only Child.
"You must terminate
the pregnancy" confuses
me
and
makes me wonder how
anyone
can understand
or care to understand
anything another
person
tries to express.

Chapter Fourteen

Spring

The hand,
muddied and draped
with weeds,
emerges from the
lake
full open;
pulling to a fist
and flexing back.
Down under—
it was down under and
mingling with the dying
leaves and fetid fish.
The winter's end
has given life. Rains
mix with the dank colors
and strain them out—
thinning the murk.
Another hand,
and then an elbow.
Shoulders and a head
climb out. Stretching
and standing on
the mud of sleep
he reaches upward—
growing in the sun.
His chest and belly,
his sex and legs are
dripping off
sheets of silt. They
run back into the lake.
Slowly he walks-
a giant from the deep-

DANSE MACABRE

    across the lake to the shore.
There he lies,
stretching every strong,
tired, and awakened muscle
on the grass and sleeps in
the sun. Breathing deeply and
exhaling through his nose.
This is how a man emerges
from the wintry sleep of sadness
and puts himself down, to rest
from his sleep. This is Spring.

GRIEF

Falling into grief
feels endless.
The helplessness
of flailing arms in
an eternal plunge
is a disconcerting
flight.
What has happened
to beauty? Beauty, the thing
that can turn flailing
into flapping
by sheer will;
change the fall into
flight.
O, Where does the
soul go now, but down?
Beauty, the steps that
give the foot a hold for
ascent. Beauty, the
muscle that pulls us
up in the soaring.
There is only descent.
Rapid and unmitigated
falling. The things
once seen as hopes,
as aspirations
have been cloaked in
the dreary gauze of mud.
Beauty no longer pulls me
up; and I fall into the muddied
pit.
Grief is about mud.

DANSE MACABRE

Smearing the brown,
wet silt all over my face,
all over my arms and trunk
and sex—right down to my legs
and feet. Down. Rolling over
and over in the downward
pulling mud. Matting
clover blossoms to
the leaves, to the
dank earth. I roll.
On my knees,
muddied and soiled
throughout,
I brush my matted hair
to the side and gaze
toward the cloud-hidden
sun and raise my hands,
crying for an end.
It is the tears,
only the tears,
that wash away
my muddied grief.

Chapter Fourteen

Down

The rain and the cold
surround my head,
dampening my ears
and brain and all
that is my soul.
Grief has not gone
so far from me
that I do not feel
her pull. My eyes
burn and pull down;
down to the dirt, to
the ground. My heart,
it sags around the edges.
The center holds firm,
but the edges sag down,
pulling to the dirt,
to the ground.
Down, down, down to
the sweet, blessed, naked
visitor grief.
She grabs all I am
and pulls me slowly
down
into the dirt,
into the ground . . .
down.

Danse Macabre

Through the Gravel

The swallow sorts
through the gravel
on the driveway
and the rain
falls. Slowly.
It falls like the
fog mist that rises
through the trees
at the suns approach.
A dance
around the light;
all of them witnesses
to the same damned play
and same glorious event.
The board watches
from the ground
where it sits,
falling apart, becoming
the very ground on
which it sits.
The dandelion watches;
sending seeds on the trail of the wind.
They go to faraway places;
parts unknown by the stem,
rooted there in the dirt.
The dirt, she watches.
She is a witness, like
the others, only it is she
who will collect back to
herself all the things that
have risen up and become—
for a time—

Chapter Fourteen

something other
than the dirt they are.
She waits for those children
to return. She watches all those
damned and glorious things
they do while they are away—
while they are separate.
All that they do
before they come home.
Like sorting through
the gravel on the driveway
as the rain falls, slowly.

DANSE MACABRE

Dirt

This body is dirt.
This body is falling apart
and crumbling up
into the dirt it is
and came from.
In 40 or 50 years I am sure
I will be found in one of those
bags of compost sold outside
the ACME. Only 2.99.
Lay me down
and spread me around
among lavender and pansies.
Put me back
where I have been
most comfortable
all my life. For I am
nothing more
than compressed
walking dirt.
I smell the basil. I see
the snapdragons, I feel
the iris bulb in my chest. I
have not left, only
changed my shape and
tried a little distance.
It won't be long. It won't
be long and I'll be back;
on the ground, in the earth;
I'll be dirt.
Sometimes
on my breath or
on my skin I can

smell the dirt. It
is then I remember who
I really am and where
I really come from. It
is then I remember
where I will end up.
But, in the end,
I often muse, where
will that part of me go;
that part of me that knows
all this—that part that
knows I'm dirt. What new
shape will that part take?
What kind of dirt will that become?
Everything changes
and comes anew. But
most things are made
of dirt.

DANSE MACABRE

A Veil of Camelot and Ease

The warmth that
fills my eyes—this
burning warmth—is
an ocean of my fears
and anxious grief. That
ocean knows
all can be lost in
the closing and opening.
A breath escapes my
nose past a heart that
is knotted with worry.
A veil of Camelot and
ease was torn while I
was celebrating.
Laughing and making merry,
I missed the sign that said,
"Danger. Do not enter."
And my life ran off the
road into the graveled shoulder,
down the embankment,
into a swamp.
Fish swim in reckless peril
in a pool of muddied waters.
Just so deep.
Shrouded by daily drying of
mud; unaware of consuming heat.
With all of the pain,
with all of the heart-ache,
it is so hard
to keep my eyes open.

MUDDIED

And,
although the river is
tumultuous and muddied
it is echoing a beauty
not often known.
A glance
and many turn,
looking the other way,
not too keen
on seeing dirt.
But,
deep within,
on the cold bottom,
the rocks sit still—
in peace.
Un-moved.

DANSE MACABRE

Like Forever

One day,
when the sun came up
like forever,
a man lost all the rage
that made him a man,
he laid it down and
became a woman.
O, He did not grow
a pair of sturdy breast—
pert and sumptuous.
He grew a softness he
never had before, he grew
tear ducts and heavy sobbings.
It was his baby's death
that gave the sunrise
its magic that day.
With
each ray of memory,
more and more of the
hardness, fell off him
in tears. Puddles of tears.
Emotion found a place
in him; it seeded in his heart.
It had come upon him
like forever.

Sobbing Dandelions
I have taken
to turning my
head
when I sob.
Usually, it is

Chapter Fourteen

to the right.
It feels outside,
away
from my heart.
I am trying to hide
the tightening I
feel going on in
the center of
my gut. I cannot.
It crawls out, slowly,
and dances around me.
In time, I become
enamored by its
dancing—it makes me
unashamed.
When I turn my head
to the left I hold the tears
inside. It is a turning
toward the center. From
there I cannot let things
out. The center is for holding.
When the season ends,
the dandelions will disappear.
There are millions of them
before the end.
But –
POOF—
all at once they end. That is
their season. And all the seeds
that have blown from all the
seeds before
will not come up
until it is their season again.
The tears will pass. Their

DANSE MACABRE

    season will end until it is their
    season again. But,
    while they are
    here,
    I will pick the tears and
    make a bouquet and carry it with pride.

Chapter Fourteen

DEATH LIKE A WEED

It has come near me again.
Quietly, like a dandelion,
it crawled into my life
and it bloomed yellow.
And, when I had finished
grieving, the wind blew
its seed deeper into me.
Who knows who will be
next, when death blooms again.
I had not seen it in
some time. Since we
planted my grandfather in
the dirt- with his moustache
and horn-rimmed glasses. Just
like mine. That was a
long time for it not to bloom.
I fear now I am mature enough
to be aware of the grief-blown-seeds.
I shall see more flowers
in shorter succession.
The trouble with weeds
is they bloom.
The trouble with blooming
 is it makes seeds.
The trouble with seeds is
they are blown about on the wind—
to find the soil,
and begin again.

DANSE MACABRE

Warmth

When the foot flattens itself
on firm, packed soil, it melts
and opens to the rays of
solar warmth. Things hold
warmth. Like a rock and
the dirt and a field of daisies.
You can feel it coming off
them. I like getting warmth
from these things. I like
getting warmth from smiling
flowers. They share it
with such love.

Chapter Fourteen

ENDINGS

You never know
what will happen at the end.
It could be anything.
The twine might be tied
to the spool, but then again
it might not. You may be
able to see the full moon,
Or she may be hidden behind
a sheet of storm clouds.
"Watch it unwind," the twine
says. "Watch and see," the
moon howls. You do not know
when you will be told to abort
your little girl, and save your wife;
or when your father will slip away;
or when the winter rain will
freeze, and turn to ice.
Watch it unwind. Look and see.

DANSE MACABRE

Quickly

Life ends so quickly.
The wind whips up over
the knoll and brushes the
roof with its endless howl.
It came from nowhere.
Not cold; no frost on the
rotting wood; no crust on
the damp grass. Wind.
Only wind. Cloud pushing,
air cleansing wind.
We buried him that day.
Another one died.
We buried him the day the
daffodils had just begun to
poke through the fallen leaves
while the wind cleared the air
and the sun shone with brilliance.
His body disappeared.
But, he will be in the wind and in the
sunshine and in the dirt and in the
tender folds of spring daffodils. He
will bring us his memory and we will
never forget.

I Do Not Understand

The earth is turning soft.
It is heaving up and being
muddy. The foot falls into it
and it sinks. These rains will
stop and the bulbs will be
pushing up through that dirt.
Death is still here. I saw it in
his skin. So tallowed, so cold,
so cold. It did not give when I
pushed it. It did not yield like the
warm jelly flesh of the living.
We walk the path that goes
through the middle. Fallen leaves
mingle with sprouting bulbs. We
are always on the path; amidst
life and death.
I do not understand it anymore.
I just weep when we die. I weep
when we are born. I pray for my
unborn daughter whose face I
did not see, whose skin I did not
touch , but whom I see and touch
in all that is.
I do not understand. But, I do know
Alex's death brought her back to me.
I will see her again,
in the silent sudden passages
from others' quietening
deaths.

DANSE MACABRE

STRANGERS

The turmoil does not leave.
It has become our guest.
We have lost our baby;
and a stranger has
entered under our roof.
The rain is falling and
the winds rip
wildly over the
muddied dirt.
Anything that is not
soaked, blows away.
Floods come and wash
and wash over and over
taking away the silt.
They have left only
my pain—our pain.
They have left only
this stranger.
Confusion rests like
the moisture in thick
clouds,
unleashing its rest
in full tempest and
subsiding again to rest.
The buds are set
on the daffodils.
Waiting.
In the wintry icy
winds and rain
and snow
they wait.
We wait, too. With
this stranger, we wait.

Chapter Fifteen

THE FEAR of death drives everything we do. All our lives are spent building up against that death. We stack beliefs, practices, impressions, attitudes, ideologies, missions, vocation, development, social patterns, interactions and every other human endeavor against the pile of "stuff and matter" that stands between us and that lemming's cliff. We pile it as high as we can against whatever it is that comes next.

The ultra-religious may say that they do not fear death, but I believe that everything we do in life is a response to addressing the idea that we are going to die someday. So, maybe we believe the Divine will take care of us, but that in itself is a response to the idea that we are going to die.

How we choose to address that fear, that anxiety, or that relationship with our ensuing death will become the legacy we leave behind. How we deal with the fact that death is stalking us at every turn is how we will be remembered as a person. And, in the end it drives the very nature and quality of the lives we are living.

Our decision to pursue consumerism and technology with all our drive and passion has cost us an immense price. We have become hollow-men who are not able to sit around and tell tales. We find stories meaningless. We struggle to stay constantly titillated by more and more sensation and ever increasing heightened experience. Without it we feel dead.

The truth is, the only thing that could possibly give us our lives back is if we sat down, looked at each other and talked about all of the things that go on inside; all of the fears and hopes that brew up in there. If we could risk enough to become human with each other, we would save ourselves by confronting the reality of our lives. If we continue to deny it and avoid it, the stuff in us will kill us. The Gospel of Thomas was correct. The desert fathers were, too. Remember that death could take you at any moment, let that inform the way you live. Tell your stories, release the garbage repressed within, and become free enough to live.

The idea of death stalks us at every turn.

It may actually be Death Himself that stalks us at every turn.

Whether it is the idea of death or Death Himself, it does not matter. We are stalked throughout our whole lives by the notion, the idea, the feeling, the reality, and the imminent haunting dream that we are going to "not be alive" someday. Someday, what we are now will either not be at all or will somehow be different—very different. We are stalked by this at every turn.

www.ingramcontent.com/pod-product-compliance
Lightning Source LLC
Chambersburg PA
CBHW050804160426
43192CB00010B/1633